MW00813647

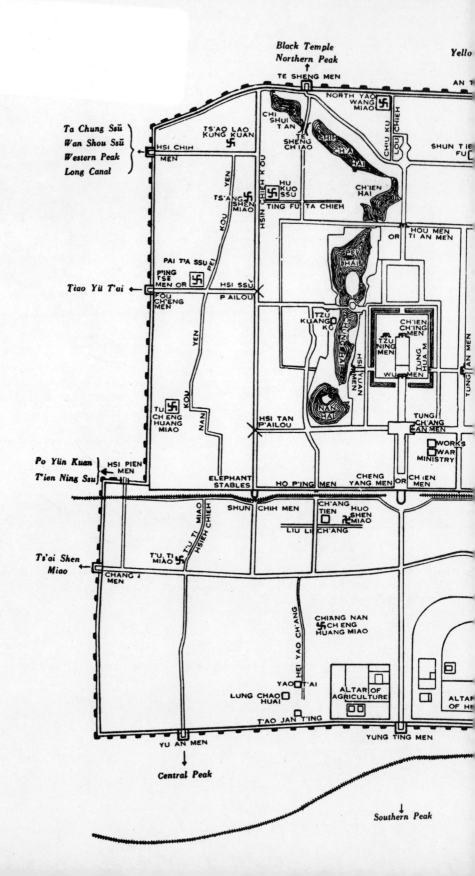

Black Temple
Northern Peak

Yello

TE SHENG MEN

AN T

NORTH YAO
WANG MIAO

Ta Chung Ssŭ
Wan Shou Ssŭ
Western Peak
Long Canal

HSI CHIH
MEN

TS'AO LAO
KUNG KUAN

CHI
SHUI
TAN

TE
SHENG
CHIAO

CHIU KU
LOU CHIEH

SHUN TIE
FU

CHIH
CHA
HAI

HSIN CHIEH K'OU

HU
KUO
SSU

CH'IEN
HAI

TS'ANG
SHEN
MIAO

TING FU TA CHIEH

HOU MEN
OR
TI AN MEN

PEI
HAI

PAI T'A SSU

P'ING
TSE
MEN OR
FOU
CH'ENG
MEN

HSI SSU
P'AILOU

Tiao Yü T'ai

TZU
KUANG
KO

CH'IEN
CH'ING
MEN

TZU
NING
MEN

TUNG
HUA M

CHUNG HAI

HSI YUAN MEN

WU MEN

TUNG AN MEN

NAN
HAI

TU
CH'ENG
HUANG
MIAO

HSI TAN
P'AILOU

TUNG
CH'ANG
AN MEN

Po Yün Kuan
T'ien Ning Ssu

HSI PIEN
MEN

WORKS
WAR
MINISTRY

ELEPHANT
STABLES

HO P'ING MEN

CHENG
YANG MEN OR

CH'IEN
MEN

SHUN CHIH MEN

CH'ANG
TIEN

HUO
SHEN
MIAO

LIU LI CH'ANG

T'U TI MIAO

Ts'ai Shen
Miao

CHANG
MEN

T'U TI
MIAO

HSIEH CHIEH

CHIANG NAN
CH'ENG
HUANG MIAO

HEI YAO CH'ANG

YAO T'AI

LUNG CHAO
HUAI

ALTAR
OF
AGRICULTURE

ALTAR
OF HE

T'AO JAN T'ING

YU AN MEN

YUNG TING MEN

Central Peak

Southern Peak

PLAN OF PEKING

INDICATING ALL PLACES WITHIN THE CITY MENTIONED IN THE BOOK

UNG HO KUNG
(LAMA TEMPLE)

SMALL
YAO WANG
MIAO

TUNG
CHIH
MEN

{ Eastern Peak
Spring Enclosure

THE ARROWS LEADING FROM THE CITY GATES POINT TOWARD PLACES IN THE SUBURBS REFERRED TO IN THE TEXT

UNG
SU
AILOU

CHI HUA
MEN OR

CHAO
YANG
MEN

→ Tung Yüeh Miao

CONVENTIONAL SIGNS

卍 TEMPLE (SSŬ, MIAO, KUAN, KUNG)

𝌆 GATE (MEN)

✕ ARCH (P'AILOU)

✕ BRIDGE (CH'IAO)

▢ PALACES, TERRACES, MINISTRIES, ETC.

→ Second Sluice

TUNG PIEN
MEN

ATAMEN OR
'UNG WEN MEN

'SAO CHUN
MIAO

P'AN
T'AO KUNG

UA-ER SHIH

0   500   1000   1500   2000 METRES

SCALE

KU'ANG
CHÜ
MEN

→ Kuan Ti
Miao

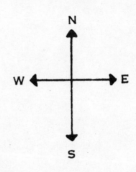

N

W ←——→ E

S

TSO AN MEN

SHUN CHIH MEN, THE WESTERNMOST OF THE FOUR SOUTHERN MAIN CITY GATES IS DESIGNATED IN THE TEXT ONLY BY ITS ALTERNATE NAME OF HSÜAN WU MEN (PP. 20, 46, 53)

ANNUAL CUSTOMS AND
FESTIVALS IN PEKING

燕京歲時記

ANNUAL
CUSTOMS AND FESTIVALS
IN PEKING

as recorded in the *Yen-ching Sui-shih-chi* by

TUN LI-CH'EN

TRANSLATED AND ANNOTATED BY

DERK BODDE

FULLY ILLUSTRATED

SECOND EDITION (REVISED)

HONG KONG UNIVERSITY PRESS
1987

First edition, Peiping 1936
Second edition, Hong Kong 1965
Second printing (with minor corrections) April 1968
Third printing March 1987

ISBN 962 209 195 4

The original edition was printed in China, by the *North-China Daily News*, Shanghai, T. D. Davy, Printer.

This reprint is an offset reproduction by
Shanghai Printing and Binding Co., 63-9 Kam Ping Street, Hong Kong.

THE GATE GOD, YÜ LEI OR HU CHING-TE

THE GATE GOD, SHEN T'U OR CH'IN CH'IUNG

See page 100

INTRODUCTION TO THE FIRST EDITION

THIS little book is a translation from the Chinese of the *Yen-ching Sui-shih-chi* 燕京歲時記, a title which literally means " Record of a Year's Time at Yen Ching," Yen Ching being an ancient name for Peking.[†] It is a record, day by day, and month by month, beginning with Chinese New Year's Day and taking us throughout the year, of what used to take place in Peking : its festivals, temple pilgrimages, fairs, customs, and the clothing, foods, and animals of the season. Many of these, of course, were peculiar to Peking, but many others were and still are widespread in China, and will have general interest, it is hoped, to all those who wish to study the popular and everyday expressions of thought of the Chinese.

The postscript of the book (see p. 105) bears a date corresponding to April 15, 1900, and though a later date of December 3, 1901, appears in the text on p. 20, it is evident that this is a supplementary note added by the author after the book as a whole had been written. This fact, and the fact that the book is written by a Manchu, have for us a special significance. They mean that in it are recorded many Manchu customs and many ceremonies of the Imperial Court which of course have utterly vanished to-day, and that the picture it gives us is that of the prosperous Peking of olden days before the great changes wrought by the disastrous Boxer Rebellion of 1900. But at the same time the work is modern enough, so that probably the greater part of what it describes is still applicable to what happens in Peking to-day.

Who was the author of this book? From its original preface, together with a brief biography appearing in the *Tzǔ-t'eng-kuan Shih-ts'ao* 紫藤館詩草, a memorial volume of his poems published after his death, we can obtain considerable information concerning his life. He belonged, as the introduction tells us, to a noble Manchu family, holding the hereditary title of Earl of Tun Hui, and his ancestors came originally from Ch'ang Pai 長白 in the province of Kirin in Manchuria. The name of his clan was Fu-ch'a 富察, his own name was Tun-ch'ung 敦崇, and his fancy name or pseudonym was Li-ch'en 禮臣. But in accordance with the usual Manchu custom, he dropped the clan name of Fu-ch'a, and gave his name a Chinese form by calling himself Tun Li-ch'en.

---

†See page xviii of the Introduction to the Second Edition.

Li-ch'en was born in 1855, so that he was already about forty-five years old when he wrote the present work.   In 1875 he wished to take the government examination, success in which would ultimately have given him official position.   But because one of his relatives was a member of the examining board, he was forced to withdraw in accordance with the usual Chinese practice, which forbade a man under such circumstances from taking the examinations, for fear that there might be unfair favoritism.   This occurred to him no less than three times, until " he became oppressed and dejected, and having no alternative, entered office by means of payment."   This practice of buying an office instead of obtaining it legitimately by passing the examinations, had long existed on a very small scale in China, but had not reached sizeable proportions until the late Manchu dynasty, beginning to feel the want of funds, had sanctioned it by Imperial Decree in 1850.

Li-ch'en thus became a petty clerk in the Ministry of War, from which he was promoted to be a Departmental Director, and later was sent to Kuangsi to be Prefect of the Ssŭ-en 思恩 Department.   Before he had arrived at his post, however, he was sent on the recommendation of the Viceroy, Hsi Liang 錫良, to be an Intendant in Manchuria.   The biography says no more of his official career, but states that in the seventh month of the third year of Hsüan T'ung (August 24 to September 21, 1911) he fell ill, and died soon after returning to Peking, at the age of fifty-seven.   His death was thus almost coincident with the outbreak of the Chinese Revolution on October 10, 1911, which was to overthrow so much which had been dear to him.

Before his death, however, Li-ch'en had succeeded in fulfilling the hope expressed in the preface to the present book, that he would " still further develop this ability, and compose other works, for the glory of those who have studied with him."   Thus his biography lists no less than ten other works from his pen, in addition to the book here translated, and the book of poems in which the biography itself appears.   These include an historical work on the *Tso Chuan*, and other books of essays, poems, and notes on Peking, etc., but all of rather a trifling nature, so that there is no doubt that it is for the present work that he will be best remembered.

From his own writing, however, considerably more can be gleaned concerning Li-ch'en's character.   Indeed, the reader of this translation will probably find it of considerable interest for the insight it gives into the Chinese thought and psychology of its author, as well as for the actual information

it gives about Chinese life and customs as a whole. For Li-ch'en is essentially
Chinese in his outlook, notwithstanding that in two places (pp. 6 and 59),
he betrays rather unnecessarily his Manchu origin by contrasting in a naïve
manner the " august frugality " of his own dynasty with the wasteful or
" childish " luxuriousness of former dynasties.

In a number of places he attains to passages of real lyric beauty which
show in a fine way Chinese human sympathy and feeling for nature. Sometimes he displays the typical, and what may seem to us exaggerated, Chinese
moral sense, as when he condemns itinerant player societies or the story-teller,
for their trouble-making proclivities (pp. 46 and 97). And at least once his
style betrays the Chinese love for literary exaggeration, as when on p. 56 he
describes " ponds of lotus whose fragrance may be smelled for several *li*."
Anyone acquainted with the lotus will know that, regardless of its other charms,
a strong fragrance is certainly not one of its characteristics.

Li-ch'en also displays a sensitive appreciation for the niceties of life, such
as one might expect in a person accustomed to luxury, yet which is characteristic, to a considerable degree, of the Chinese people as a whole. Thus it would
be hard to find any European or American gentleman, not himself a special
breeder of pigeons, who could recite the long list of varieties of pigeons given
by our author on pp. 21-22 ; and still harder to find any European or American
who could write down the list of varieties of chrysanthemums (even if
the names are poetical rather than ones actually used), given on pp. 71-73,
of which our author says in conclusion : " This makes a total of one hundred
and thirty-three kinds, all of which I remember. But for those who can think
of them, there are still more than two hundred other kinds. . . . . . "

Yet Li-ch'en was more than a mere æsthete. In his section on crickets
(p. 82) he speaks of the inordinate craze for elaborate cricket cages as
one of the causes leading to the impoverishment of so many of Peking's nobles.
And in his section on the " pacing-horse " lantern (pp. 80-81), one of the most
interesting in the book, with its ingenious analogy of the Chinese concept
of history to a children's toy, he shows a keen awareness of the problems of
the unscientific and non-industrialized China of his time, facing an industrialized
West, and attacks whole-heartedly China's self-complacency. Again, on p. 19,
he mentions the fact that he has read western books on agriculture. There
is one other reference on p. 18 to the West, by the way, in which he makes
the interesting statement that already in his time " as to old porcelain, it is
extremely scarce, for much of it has already been bought and taken away by
foreigners."

Yet why, it may still be asked, should such a book as this be translated, when there are already books by westerners on the subject? The answer is that it is valuable because it gives an account, in a concise and straightforward manner, of Chinese life and customs as a Chinese himself would look at them. It avoids those two besetting sins of foreign books on the subject: either a tendency to sentimentalize in a way which is western rather than Chinese, and which tends to throw a wrong coloring on what is described; or to compile a bulky disquisition so learned and profound as to repel the average reader. At the same time it is valuable because it gives a large amount of information, culled from earlier Chinese sources, describing the origins of various festivals and antiquities.

There is one rather striking feature of our book, which is that within its pages the name of Confucius is not once directly mentioned; only on p. 10 is he incidentally referred to as "The Sage," in a literary quotation. This fact is significant and important as indicating that Confucianism, regardless of the part it has played in molding the thought and morality of China's ruling and educated classes, has after all had comparatively little impact on the ideology of her common people, to such extent, at least, as this has become concretely manifested in customs and festivals. Buddhism has played a greater part, though here too we find only three customs which are specifically Buddhist: the distribution of beans on the eighth day of the fourth month; All Souls' Day on the fifteenth of the seventh month; and the *la pa* gruel offerings on the eighth day of the twelfth month. And even here, these last two probably go back to pre-Buddhist origins.

Taoism, in its religious rather than philosophical aspects, with its many temples dedicated to the God of T'ai Shan, and his daughter, the Princess of the Colored Clouds, has been of greater importance. Yet we must go beyond these organized religions, to the cult of the local or historical deities such as the God of War or the City Gods; to that of the tutelary deities, such as the God of the Kitchen, long preceding either Taoism or Buddhism; and above all to the form in which Chinese religious feeling has most beautifully expressed itself — that of the worship of ancestors — to reach the true heart of the common people.

What will perhaps most strike the reader is to observe how closely so many of the festivals are associated with nature. These begin in the first month with the worship of stars and the Lantern Festival, and continue in early

spring with the *Ch'ing Ming* festival, which takes the people out into the countryside to the graves of their ancestors. And just as in Chaucer's England

> Whan that Aprille with his shoures soote
> The droghte of March hath perced to the roote,
>
> . . . .
>
> Thanne longen folk to goon on pilgrimages,

so in China the third and fourth months are times when pilgrimages are made
to many temples lying amidst the most beautiful natural surroundings ; and
made with the same joy and gaiety which characterized the Canterbury
Pilgrims. Several other festivals are likewise intimately associated with the
forces of nature, and it is interesting to note that no less than three of these,
the Lantern Festival, All Souls' Day, and the Moon Festival, come at the time
of, and are closely connected with, the full moon.

There is a great deal here that is beautiful and worthy of our admiration,
and only a little (perhaps only the account on p. 46 of the penances performed
during the tour made by the God of the City), which is repellent. Indeed,
what the translator has felt most strongly in making this translation, and what
he hopes his readers will feel, is the sentiment here indirectly expressed of the
essential oneness and harmony of man with the universe. It is a sentiment
which permeates much of the greatest Chinese art and poetry, for in the Chinese,
as perhaps in no other people, has been developed a keen consciousness and
awareness of the movement and rhythm of nature, as evidenced in the yearly
rotation of the seasons. It is an awareness which has made them deliberately
subordinate their own activities to that of the forces of nature, so that as we
read this book, we find such things as their foods, the clothes which they put
on, and the lighting and taking away of their winter fires, all following in
their times a course as rigid as that of the birds in their seasonal migrations.

Perhaps it is this subordination of man's will which has prevented China
from achieving a science, for science is born from the struggle against, rather
than the submission to, natural forces. But in its place it has given a spiritual
calm which has carried the Chinese unshaken through the severest trials, and
if some realization of this fact can herein be conveyed to western readers,
this book will not have failed to do its bit to help in the understanding of the
heart of a great people.

To-day, with the advent of industrialism, and the accompanying influx
of standardized ways of life, this consciousness of nature tends to die,
together with the beautiful customs it has engendered. It is left for the
reader to judge who is the gainer and who the loser.

A few words as to the method of translation may not be out of place here. The edition used has been that of the *Wen Te Chai* 文德齋, published in Peking in 1906. The translator has tried hard to avoid that Scylla and Charybdis of translators of Chinese books : the making of the translation so exact and scientific that the average reader, who knows nothing about Chinese, and who wishes to be entertained as well as informed, will never look at it ; and making it so superficial and loose that it will meet only condemnation from the scholar. He hopes that he has succeeded in producing a text smooth enough to please the former, and yet close enough to the original to satisfy the latter. Single words which the author obviously intends, but which the original text omits because they are not required by the exigencies of Chinese style, the translator has not hesitated to add. Anything more elaborate than this, however, such as an interpretation offered by the translator of what the author probably implies but does not directly express, or something supplied to give clarity to the western reader, has been added enclosed in parentheses. Thus everything within parentheses, and all notes, both those embodied in the text, giving general explanations, and the footnotes, dealing with detailed points, are by the translator. The only exception to this are the three or four notes made by the author himself, which are marked *Author's Note*.

Very little of the original text has been left untranslated, save the fairly numerous poems, stone-tablet inscriptions, etc., which it contains, and which were not composed by the author himself, but commonly by Emperors or other persons of high degree. These are usually written in such flowery language that a satisfactory translation of them would be extremely difficult, and would add little to the interest of the book. Aside from these, a few other passages have been omitted, usually those which have only a philological interest, or which discuss places already described in other books on Peking. These omissions are rare, and when more than a few words long, are explained in the footnotes. But if the omission is less than a sentence in length, it is simply indicated in the usual way by a series of periods. . . . . In order not to crowd the text with Chinese characters, an index has been prepared where all the important Chinese names and words will be found.

As to the illustrations, all the wood engravings have been taken from the *Hung-hsüeh Yin-yüan-t'u-chi* 鴻雪因緣圖記, a book in six volumes, the various prefaces to which bear dates ranging from 1839 to 1849. This was also written, fittingly enough, by a Manchu, Lin Ch'ing 麟慶, who for ten years was a General Inspector of the Imperial Canals, and in this post travelled to many parts of China, making, as he did so, short descriptions of the spots he visited, and illustrations to go with them. Some of his illustrations dealing with Peking appear here. The sketches are by Mr. Fu Shu-ta 傅叔達, of Peiping.

It is a pleasure to acknowledge the help of the many persons who have contributed to this translation. First among them comes Mr. Sun Shih-hsün 孫世訓, a fine old gentleman of the old school, without whose wide knowledge of the Peking of former times, the making of this translation would have been far more difficult. Others to whom deep thanks are due are Professor Chang Hsing-lang 張星烺, Head of the Department of History of the Catholic University, Peiping, for much information on Chinese terms and phrases ; Dr. John C. Ferguson, who read the proofs and gave many valuable suggestions ; Mr. L. C. Arlington, well-known co-author of *In Search of Old Peking*, for information concerning certain places in Peking ; Mr. S. A. Polevoy, translator of a book of Mongol fairy stories into Chinese, for certain Manchu terms ; Dean William Hung 洪業, of the Harvard-Yenching Institute at Yenching University, Peiping, for bibliographical information ; Mr. Henri Vetch, who did all he could to help the book through the press ; Messrs. Chang Ch'un-ling 張春霖, Hu Hsien-hsiu 胡先驌, Li Liang-ch'ing 李良慶, and Shou Chen-huang 壽振璜, of the Fan Memorial Institute of Biology, Peiping, for the western equivalents of certain Chinese names of plants, birds, and fish ; and last, but not least, the translator's mother and wife, for reading the manuscript and giving many helpful suggestions.

DERK BODDE

PEIPING, CHINA,
SEPTEMBER 21, 1935.

INTRODUCTION TO THE SECOND EDITION

WHEN, in the spring of 1900, Tun Li-ch'en 敦禮臣 completed his *Yen-ching Sui-shih-chi* 燕京歲時記, it is most unlikely that he in any way envisaged the long series of changes to his beloved Peking which were to begin with the Boxer Rebellion only a few weeks hence. Some thirty-five years later, when this writer was translating Li-ch'en's book into English, he, like many other Western students then in Peking, succeeded in ignoring the threats of coming crisis and burying himself happily in the old ways of life which, to a remarkable degree and despite all change, still prevailed there during those last golden years.

The writer was in Manila en route to Europe when, on 7 July 1937, little more than a year after *Annual Customs* was published, he saw the newspaper headlines proclaiming the clash between Chinese and Japanese soldiers at the Marco Polo Bridge outside Peking. This incident, marking the Asian beginning of World War II, also marked the final beginning of the end for the old Peking. In 1948, when the writer returned there again, what he found was a sad and impoverished city—one whose people were too busy struggling for survival to bother about tradition.

Today the city is no longer sad and impoverished, but pulses with new life. For this very reason, Tun Li-ch'en would undoubtedly find difficulty in recognizing it. Innumerable large new buildings pierce what was once a uniform skyline, much or most of the city wall has been torn down, and the city itself has spilled into the surrounding countryside to engulf many of the temples and monuments described in Tun's book. It can hardly be doubted that what he recorded in 1900, and what in good part still survived in the 1930's, has now either disappeared for all time or has been changed into something almost unrecognizable.

That those of us who loved the old Peking should be saddened by this fact is but natural, but we should not on this account feel bitter. Many of us were foreigners whose standard of living, if modest in our own eyes, was far higher than that of the great bulk of the Chinese population. A native way of life which to us as outsiders seemed picturesque and quaint was to the indigenous rickshaw coolie or beggar mostly bitter and often individually short. Today the picturesque quaintness has left Peking, but the rickshaw coolie, the beggar, and countless other deprived persons have vanished also. Though life in modern China, judged by Western standards, still remains infinitely below what it is for most people in the West, it is unlikely that many Chinese today would willingly return to the 'good old times' of picturesque poverty, dirt, disease, and famine, any more than many Americans would willingly exchange their automobiles and TVs for the simpler pleasures of the pre-automobile age.

The troubles breaking over China soon after the publication of *Annual Customs* prevented the book from achieving a wide distribution and caused it, within a few years, to become totally unavailable. It is highly gratifying, therefore, that now, three decades later, when the contents of the book possess only historical significance, there should nevertheless be sufficient interest in this, the writer's first book-length venture into Chinese scholarship, to warrant its republication. Particularly gratifying is the fact that this republication is being done by the book's original publisher, Henri Vetch, from whom the writer, in his student days, learned so much both about book writing and about book publishing.[1]

Were the translator to do this book now instead of thirty years ago, he no doubt could make the translation more literal and the foot-notes more detailed, thereby eliciting praise from scholars. It by no means necessarily follows, however, that the book would thereby become more attractive to the general interested reader for whom, after all, it was originally primarily intended. Be that as it may, the translator hopes that today he would no longer be capable of a factual error which, unknown to readers of the book until now, seriously mars its opening pages.

In 1941, when Peking was the seat of the Japanese-controlled puppet government of North China, a Japanese scholar, Ono Katsutoshi 小野勝年, published a Japanese translation of Tun Li-ch'en's Chinese opus under the title, *Peking nenjū gyōji-ki* 北京年中行事記 ('Tōkyō: Iwanami Book Co., 1941, 282 small pages). In so doing he may have been inspired to some extent by the English translation, from which he quotes at length in several places. On the whole, the Japanese translation is a very good piece of work. Its notes are fuller than those of the English translation, particularly with regard to historical, biographical, and literary references, though they show less personal knowledge of Peking than does the English version. At the end of the Japanese text comes a reprint of the Chinese original, with suggestions for various textual emendations, not all of which, by any means, seem valid.

In 1942, when Chou Tso-jen 周作人, brother of the famous writer Lu Hsün, was Minister of Education in the puppet Peking government, he was inspired by these two translations to write a comparative review of them in Chinese. The review appeared in an obscure and probably short-lived journal, *Kuo-li Hua-pei Pien-yi-kuan Kuan-k'an* 國立華北編譯館館刊 (Journal of the National North China Translation Bureau), Vol. I, No. 1 (October 1, 1942), first four pages of the book review section.[2]

---

[1] Another very rare book about Peking which richly deserves republication, not because it is highly scholarly, but because it is charmingly written and illustrated, and contains quantities of authentic information about life in old Peking not otherwise readily obtainable, is H. Y. Löwe, *The Adventures of Wu: The Life Cycle of a Peking Man*, 2 vols. (Peking: Peking Chronicle Press, 1940-41).

[2] The review is signed Yao-t'ang 藥堂, which is one of Chou Tso-jen's many pen-names. At the end of World War II, Chou was imprisoned as a war criminal, but today, according to recent reports, he lives in freedom in Peking, where in 1963 he published a Chinese translation of the ancient Japanese historical work, *Kojiki*. This information comes from Mr. Howard L. Boorman, Director of the Research Project on Men and Politics in Modern China. To him I am deeply indebted for locating the journal containing the Chou review in Columbia University's East Asian Library, and (with the kind co-operation of Dr. T. K. Tong of that Library) supplying me with photostats of the review. To Professor John K. Fairbank of Harvard I am likewise profoundly indebted for not only informing me, more than a decade ago, of the Chou review, but also generously presenting me with a copy of the Japanese translation by Ono Katsutoshi.

Though Chou's review mentions several errors in both translations, what makes it really important is its new information about Tun Li-ch'en himself. In the present writer's 1935 introduction to *Annual Customs* (p. vii above), he gave Li-ch'en's death date as 1911, basing himself upon biographical information contained in the slim volume of Li-ch'en's poems known as the *Tzŭ-t'eng-kuan Shih-ts'ao* 紫藤館詩草. However, the relevant passage in this volume, as quoted by Chou, states merely that Li-ch'en, because of illness, returned to Peking in the seventh lunar month of 1911, and that subsequent to the outbreak of the Revolution shortly thereafter, he did not again leave his house, except to attend the funeral of the Empress Dowager Lung-yü (the widow of the Kuang-hsü Emperor). As pointed out by Chou, this funeral occurred in 1913. How, therefore, the present writer could ever have concluded that Li-ch'en's 1911 illness was fatal, remains to him a mystery.

Equally mysterious is the version of events given in the Japanese translation. This says that when the former Hsüan-t'ung Emperor (Henry P'u-yi) married in 1922, Tun Li-ch'en committed suicide by drowning himself in the canal at Pa-li-ch'iao 八里橋 (Eight *Li* Bridge), east of Peking on the canal leading to Tungchow. To rebut this completely unsupported assertion, Chou Tso-jen quotes from a short volume of literary pieces by Li-ch'en (probably extant in manuscript form only), the *Hua-hu chi-wen ch'ao* 畫虎集文鈔. At the end of this volume appears a preface by Li-ch'en written for a collection of poems by a friend and called "Preface to the Poems of the Recluse Old Gentleman Chou Yü-chih of Chieh-shih" 碣石逸叟周鏡之詩序. In this preface, Li-ch'en clearly refers to himself as an old man of seventy suffering from illness. He states that he is writing the preface on New Year's Day of the *chia-tzŭ* year, a date corresponding to 5 February, 1924.

There is no doubt, then, that Tun Li-ch'en was born in 1855, and that he died neither in 1911 nor in 1922, but was still alive, despite illness, at the beginning of 1924. Thereafter nothing more is heard of him. Probably he died not long afterward.

In preparing this new edition of *Annual Customs*, it was not feasible to make a thoroughgoing revision of the text. The only completely altered section is Appendix F, wherein what had been 'Concordance of Lunar and Western Calendar from 1936 to 1956' now becomes the same 'from 1957 to 1984'. A fair number of lesser typographical errors (many of them minor romanization errors) have been corrected directly in the text, wherein lengthier corrections or additions have also, when feasible, been made (see especially notes on pp. 22, 88, 112 and 128). Still other corrections, which could not thus be fitted in, are listed below under the following Corrigenda. Some come from the translator himself, others from the following reviews or personal communications on the first edition—identified by name under each item of the Corrigenda to which they are relevant or at the end of the additional footnote material inserted directly in the main text.

Herbert Chatley (now deceased), personal letter of 12 July 1936
Chou Tso-jen, review cited above
J. J. L. Duyvendak (now deceased), review in *T'oung Pao*, **33** (1937): 102-104
John C. Ferguson (now deceased), personal letter of 18 July 1936
Hermann Köster, review in *Monumenta Serica*, **2** (1936-37): 225-226
Arthur Waley, review in *Folklore*, **47** (1936): 402-403

Corrigenda

vii. The Chinese title of the book, *Yen-ching Sui-shih-chi*, does not, as here asserted, mean 'Record of a Year's Time at Yen Ching'. The title really signifies: 'Record of the Annual Seasons (*sui-shih* 歲時) at Yen Ching'. [Duyvendak]

3. 'Day for Human Beings': *for* According to the ancient writings of Tung-fang So *perhaps read* According to the *Chan Shu* 占書 (Book of Prognosticauons) of Tung-fang So . . . [Suggested in Japanese translation, p. 29, on the ground that Tung-fang So was in fact author of a *Chan Shu*, now lost, and that the phrase *ku shu* 古書, translated from the text as 'ancient writings', might easily be a graphic confusion for *Chan Shu*.]

5. Beginning of lower paragraph: *for* the magistrates . . . having stationed themselves outside the Wu Men *read* the magistrates . . . having set up a table (on which to offer sacrifices) outside the Wu Men. [Köster]

6. Add to upper *Note:* Probably the real origin of the practice lies in the belief, anciently widespread, that the bull is the concentrated essence of virility, and that therefore by beating (originally slaying) him in spring, when life annually renews itself, one will acquire the bull's virility. See, for example, Carl W. Bishop, 'The Ritual Bullfight', *China Journal*, **3** (1925): 630-637; reprinted in *Smithsonian Institution Annual Report for 1926*, pp. 447-456.

15. Line 2: *for* of the Palace of the Great Ultimate *read* of the Yüan dynasty Palace of the Great Ultimate. [Köster]

18. Paragraph 2, lines 4-5: *for* Director of the Ministry of Works *read* Departmental Director in the Ministry of Works. [Köster]

22. Middle paragraph, line 3 from bottom: *for* Truly it gives joy *read* Truly it gives joy to the ear.

28. Add to first *Note:* For another more scholarly and more up-to-date study of Hsi Wang Mu, see H. H. Dubs, 'An Ancient Chinese Mystery Cult', *Harvard Theological Review*, **35** (1942): 221-240.

43. First line: *for* closed with lily leaves *read* closed with leaves of the Persian lilac *(Melia Azedarach)*. [Chou Tso-jen suggests that the translator made this mistake by confusing the text's *lien* 楝 (Persian lilac) with *lien* 蓮 (lily).]

63. Line 5: *for* give offerings to these lonely gods *read* give offerings to the lonely ones (i.e., lonely spirits of the departed). [As pointed out by Chou Tso-jen, the City Gods all have wives and attendants, so that they cannot be spoken of as "lonely" (*ku* 孤). What this term surely refers to, therefore, is the spirits of dead persons who have no families to care for them. This is strongly implied by the statement in the text that the offerings to these lonely ones are made on *Chung Yüan*, on *Ch'ing Ming*, and on the first day of the tenth month, all of which are days of offerings to the departed.]

75. Add to *Note:* In all probability, however, *tou-ni-ku-to* is a corruption of *tüntük*, a Mongol word which means 'meat dumplings'. [Waley]

76. First two paragraphs: Despite Tun Li-ch'en's distinction between the two, there is little real difference between *pu-hui-mu*, translated 'amianthus', and the classical Chinese term for asbestos used by Tun Li-ch'en below, *huo-wan pu* 火浣布 (lit., 'cloth washable in fire'), translated as 'asbestos cloth'. In line 1, 'the inner part of fossils' is a mistranslation of *hua-shih ken* 化 (=滑) 石根, which means 'the root of soapstone'. This term appears in an XI century text, where it is used to express the correct fact that asbestos commonly occurs in conjunction with soapstone. See Joseph Needham, *Science and Civilisation in China*, **3** (Cambridge, 1959): 655-662, esp. 656 and 660.

97. Line 2: *ju kuang ling san* 如廣陵散 does not mean 'they have disappeared like Kuang Ling' but 'they have become like Kuang-ling-san' (i.e., they have totally come to an end). Kuang-ling-san was the name of a musical air which supposedly was the favourite of the famed poet and musician Hsi K'ang 嵇康 (A.D. 223-262), and which he is said to have

played on his lute at the moment of his unjust execution, when, of course, his playing of it was cut off for all time. See R. H. van Gulik, *Hsi K'ang and His Poetical Essay on the Lute* (Tōkyō: Sophia University, 1941): 22, 31-34. [Chou Tso-jen and Japanese translation, p. 199, note 6.]

103. 'Cash to Pass the Year': The text's *ya sui ch'ien* 壓歲錢, 'cash to pass the year', involves a play on words with *ya sui* 素 *ch'ien*, 'cash to press down evil influences', or again with *ya* 押 *sui ch'ien*, 'cash serving as a pledge for the year'. [Duyvendak, citing Wilhelm Grube, *Zur Pekinger Volkskunde* (Berlin, 1901): 48.]

107. Table of 24 solar 'sections' or 'joints': For 6, 'Corn Rain', read 'Grain Rain'; for 8, 'Grain Full', read 'Small Fullness of Grain'; for 9, 'Grain in the Ear', read 'Grain in Beard'. In line 3 of the text above, 'every fifteen days' should be corrected to 'approximately every fifteen days', since the average space of time between any two of the joints is slightly more than 15 days (actually 15·22 days). The correlations of the twenty-four solar periods with the dates in the lunar (and therefore fluctuating) calendar are inexact. It would be better simply to correlate the first two periods with the first lunar month, the next two with the second month, and so through the series, ending with periods 23 and 24 which go with the twelfth month. [Dr Chatley suggested all the above corrections save the new renditions for 'Corn Grain' and 'Grain Full'.]

108. Line 4: *for* 163 B.C. *read* 114 or 113 B.C. [This is the time when the concept of reign periods actually originated. What purport to be earlier reign periods were in actual fact established only retroactively at a later date. See H. H. Dubs, *History of the Former Han Dynasty*, **2** (Baltimore, 1944): 121-122.]

130. *Shih-shih Yao-lan:* This can be more precisely dated by its preface, which bears a date corresponding to 1020. The work is No. 2127 in the Taishō edition of the Chinese version of the Buddhist *Tripiṭaka.*

130. *Yen-tu Yu-lan-chih:* This work, originally in 40 *chüan*, is now no longer extant. Our text cites it as quoted in the *Jih-hsia*, *chüan* 148. [Japanese translation, p. 193, note 3.]

130. *Yüeh-ling Kuang-i:* Feng Ying-ching's precise dates are 1555-1606.

DERK BODDE

Philadelphia, U.S.A.

26 January 1965

Professor of Chinese

University of Pennsylvania

CONTENTS

ILLUSTRATIONS

PLATES

DRAWINGS IN THE TEXT

ORIGINAL PREFACE

My friend, Tun Li-ch'en 敦禮臣, is a member of a noble Manchu family, being a descendant in the eighth generation of the Grand Tutor and Grand Secretary, Duke Wen Mu 文穆公 of the Ma 馬 family. He inherits the title of Earl of Tun Hui 敦惠伯, and is the second son of Ch'eng Chien-t'ang 承簡堂, squire. As boys we were fellow-students, both of us receiving our education from Wu Shao-yün 烏紹雲, President of the Ministry of Works. Li-ch'en was the latter's nephew, so that his is a far-reaching origin indeed. His intelligence surpasses that of other men, while in the practice of the literary arts he is also able to make a good showing, so that his associates have conceded him an ability such as is worthy of being marketed.

At the special examination held through Imperial kindness in the *Yi-hai* year (1875), I and my brother both received the degree of *hsiang chien*,[1] but Li-ch'en, because one of his relatives (was among those in charge of the examinations), had to withdraw, and hence was not allowed even once to offer his " ox cleaver."[2] What a pity indeed! Several times later on he again was forced to withdraw, so that he became oppressed and dejected, and, having no other alternative, entered office by means of payment, something which he had never intended doing.

In the leisure time after meals he continued to amuse himself with books and histories, so that he had a wide knowledge of the origin of many of the antiquities of the present dynasty. Thus one day when I happened to pass his place, I saw on a table his *Yen-ching Sui-shih-chi*, in one volume. I took it up and read it through once, which was enough to show to me his imaginative mind. Although this is not a grand production nor a vast literary work,

---

[1] 鄉薦, i.e., the second or *chü jen* 舉人 degree in the government examinations.

[2] This expression has reference to the *Lun Yü* (Confucian Analects), XVII, 4, in which it is said of Confucius : " When the Master came to Wu-ch'eng he heard (everywhere) the sound of string instruments and singing ; whereupon he smiled and laughingly said, ' Why use an ox cleaver to kill a chicken ? ' ' A while ago, Sir,' replied Tzŭ Lŭ (a disciple), ' I heard you say : When men of rank have learnt morality they love their fellow-men ; and when the common people have learnt morality, they are easily commanded.' ' My disciples ! ' said the Master, ' Yen's remark is right. What I said before was only in jest.' " Hence the expression here of " ox cleaver " means that Tun Li-ch'en, with his unusual ability (the " ox cleaver "), would have had no difficulty in passing the examination.

it will serve indeed to contribute to investigations made in the future (into the old customs), its purpose thus being the same as that of the (*Ti-ching*) *Ching-wu-lüeh* and the (*Pei-ching*) *Sui-hua-chi*.[1]

But even so, how can the learning of such a man as Li-ch'en stop with this? I hope that he will still further develop this ability, and compose other works, for the glory of those who have studied with him. This indeed is my fervent hope.

This introduction is respectfully presented in the *Chia-p'ing* month of the *Chi-hai* year, twenty-fifth year of Kuang Hsü (January 11 to February 10, 1900), by a stupid elder fellow-student, Jun-fang Shu-t'ien 潤芳澍田, on whom has been conferred the degree of *chin shih*,[2] and who holds the office of Second Assistant Secretary in the Ministry of Justice.

The characters have been respectfully written by Ch'ing-chen Po-ju 慶珍博如, a younger male relative through marriage, of the fourth official rank,[3] with the decoration of a peacock feather, and who holds the position of Assistant Director in the Ministry of War.

---

[1] For these, and all other books mentioned in the text, see the Bibliography.

[2] 進 士, the third degree in the government examinations.

[3] Under the Manchu dynasty there were nine grades of officials, distinguished by the buttons of jade and of other stones put on their Mandarin hats.

CHAPTER I—THE FIRST MONTH

New Year's Day (*Yüan Tan* 元旦)

In Peking the first day of the year is called the *Yüan Tan*, and on each first day, from the *tzŭ* period onward (i.e., the period extending from eleven p.m. of New Year's Eve to one a.m. of New Year's Morning), incense is burned to meet the spirits (who descend to earth at this time), and fire-crackers are lighted to show them respect, so that their noise fills the streets unceasingly throughout the night. After the greeting of the spirits everyone, from princes and dukes down to the various officials, must enter the Palace to offer congratulations to the Court ; and on the conclusion of these Court felicitations, they go about paying visits to their relatives and friends, this being called wishing New Year Happiness (*hsin hsi* 新喜). Close relatives actually enter the reception halls themselves, while those who are unrelated simply leave their cards. Clothed in furs of sable and ceremonial embroidered robes, they mill confusedly about the streets, their carriages truly like flowing water, and their horses like roaming dragons, in their numbers ! It is a spectacle indeed of universal welfare and prosperity !

Everyone on this day, whether rich or poor, of noble or humble rank, makes dumplings out of white flour and eats them, and these are called boiled *po-po* 餑餑. Throughout the entire country it is thus ; nowhere is it different. In rich and noble homes such things as small pieces of gold and silver or precious stones are secretly put inside the *po-po*, so as to foretell who is to have prosperity. Thus to those members of the family who while eating get these things, there will be great good fortune throughout the year.

According to the *Ching-ch'u Sui-shih-chi*, on the first day of the first month " bursting bamboos " [1] are first of all lighted in front of the

---

[1] *Pao chu* 爆竹. Before gunpowder was known, sections of bamboo were thrown into fire, so that the heat would cause them to explode with a loud sound. Later this term has come to mean ordinary fire-crackers.

main hall, so as to ward off the " mountain stenches " [1] and evil spirits. Again, according to the *Yü-chu Pao-tien*, the first day of the first month is called the Day of Beginning (*Yüan Jih* 元 日), and is also called the Three Beginnings : that of the year, of the season, and of the month.

PURSES OF THE 'EIGHT TREASURES' (*Pa Pao* 八 寶)

On every New Year's Day all the princes, dukes, and great officials whose activities lie within the Palace, as well as the Guards of the Ante-Chamber, etc., are presented by the Emperor with purses embroidered with the eight treasures, which they hang on their chests. But the great officials of the Ministries and Departments outside the Palace do not have this custom.

Note : These eight treasures are the eight Buddhist symbols : the Wheel of the Law, Conch-shell, Umbrella, Canopy, Lotus, Jar, Fish, and the Mystic Knot.

THE 'EIGHT TREASURES'

WORSHIP OF THE 'GOD OF WEALTH' (*Ts'ai Shen* 財 神)

On the second day comes the worship of the God of Wealth, when fire-crackers are extremely numerous, never ceasing day or night.

Note : This god, whose prototype is said to have been one of several historical persons of various periods, is one of the most popular, so that he is worshipped both in private homes and in temples dedicated to him. *Cf.* p. 74.

---

[1] *Shan sao* 山臊. This term occurs in the *Shen-i-ching* 神異經, a book of marvels dating from probably the fourth or fifth century A.D. (*cf.* Wylie, *Notes on Chinese Literature*, 191), which has the passage : " In the west amidst the deep mountains are men whose bodies are somewhat more than one foot in height. Their bodies are naked and they grasp crabs. By their nature they do not fear (ordinary) men, and when they see people stopping for the night, they make use of their fires during the evening to roast the crabs. Their name is *shan sao*."

Breaking the Five (P'o Wu 破五)

The fifth day of the month is called the *P'o Wu*. Before this day it is not permitted to cook fresh rice, (all delicacies having been prepared beforehand for the New Year), nor are women permitted to leave their homes. But upon the sixth day princesses and royal daughters, together with their entourage, put on their head-dresses and capes, and come and go, offering congratulations to one another. Also newly married women upon this day pay a visit to their parental homes. The vernal days are now mild, and the spring clay softens into slush. Gay carriages with their embroidered canopies block the lanes and fill up the big streets. And now, too, merchants of the market-places little by little open their shops and begin business.

Day for Human Beings (Jen Jih 人日)

The seventh day is called the Day for Human Beings, and if on that day the weather is clear and bright, human births will be prolific (during the coming year). According to the ancient writings of Tung-fang So,[1] the eight days following the beginning of the year are : the first, the day of chickens ; the second, that of dogs ; the third, that of pigs ; the fourth, that of sheep ; the fifth, that of oxen ; the sixth, that of horses ; the seventh, that of human beings ; the eighth, that of grains. If these days are clear and bright, the creatures born under their respective influences will mature. But if the days are dark, these creatures will suffer disaster.

Homage to the Stars (Shun Hsing 順星)

On the eighth day (in some provinces on the eighteenth), after twilight, one hundred and eight lamps are lighted, made out of paper tapers soaked in oil, while incense is burned and offered. This is called the *Shun Hsing*. From the thirteenth to the sixteenth day, lamps are again lighted and burn brightly, extending from the south-west corner of the main hall to the main gate. This is called " scattering

---

[1] Born 160 B.C., he was a Censor under Emperor Wu Ti of the Han dynasty, and was noted for his wit. The *Shen-i-ching* (*cf.* preceding Note) has been attributed to him, but probably erroneously.

lantern flowers," or again, " scattering small men," and is done with the idea of warding off the inauspicious.

According to the *Ti-ching Ching-wu-lüeh*, on the thirteenth day of the first month each household would take one hundred and eight small lamp cups, light them at night, and scatter them on the well, the kitchen stove, the gates, the doors, and the stone block on which clothing is beaten while washed, this being called the " scattering of the lamps." Grouped together, they would look like fireflies ; scattered, like stars. Rich people would light them during four evenings, poor people for only one evening, while the extremely poor did not have this custom.

What is here recorded is in a general way identical with the custom to-day, but I have not succeeded in obtaining details about it.

> *Note*: There is an interesting combination in this account of a general worship to the many star gods, together with the ancient worship of the five tutelary gods of the house : those of the kitchen stove ; of gates ; doors ; the center of the room or impluvium ; and the well or, according to some, the alleys. This worship dates from before the time of Christ. *Cf.* Legge's translation of the *Li Chi* (Book of Rites) in *Sacred Books of the East*, XXVII, 116. In the present ceremony, however, the washing stone has replaced the impluvium.

' BEATING OF THE SPRING ' (*Ta Ch'un* 打春)

> *Author's Note*: This festival (being regulated by the solar rather than the lunar calendar) does not fall on any fixed day (of the lunar month), and so is simply recorded as occurring during the first month. Other festivals of this kind will also follow this arrangement.

The " Beating of the Spring " is the same as the Beginning of Spring (*Li Ch'un* 立春), and usually occurs during the first month. One day preceding the Beginning of Spring, the officials of the Metropolitan Prefecture (the governmental organ which had jurisdiction over the Capital) proceed one *li* outside Tung Chih Men to the Spring Enclosure to welcome in the spring.[1] At the Beginning of Spring the Ministry of Rites presents to the Emperor a Spring-hill Throne (*ch'un shan pao tso* 春山寶座) and the Metropolitan Prefecture presents an effigy of a Spring Ox (*ch'un niu* 春牛).[2] On

---

[1] This ceremony goes back to very early times. *Cf.* the description in the *Li Chi*, Legge's translation in *Sacred Books of the East*, XXVII, 253 f.

[2] For an ancient account of this ox, which was at first made of clay, and in later times of paper, *cf. Li Chi, op. cit.*, p. 307. The Spring-hill Throne is probably for the Mang Shen (*cf.* Note on p. 5), or perhaps for the Year God (T'ai Sui 太歲), i.e., the god of the planet Jupiter, who has control over time.

the conclusion of the ceremony they return to their offices, leading the Spring Ox along and beating it, this being called the " Beating of the Spring."

On this same day many rich families eat " spring cakes " (*ch'un ping* 春 餅), and women all buy turnips and eat them, which is termed " gnawing the spring " (*chiao ch'un* 咬 春), meaning that thereby the fatigues of spring may be warded off.

According to what is recorded in the *Li-pu Tse-li*, on the day preceding the Beginning of Spring, the Prefect of the Metropolitan Prefecture with his accompanying officials and followers, would, all in Court robes, welcome in the spring outside Tung Chih Men. Their assistants would raise up the Mang Shen 芒 神 and the Earth Ox (i.e., Spring Ox), and to the sound of drums conduct them to the front of their offices, where they put them out under a colored silk covering.[1]

At the Beginning of Spring, the magistrates of the districts of Ta Hsing and Wan P'ing (districts in which Peking is situated), having stationed themselves outside the Wu Men (the main entrance to the Forbidden City), directly in the center, would respectfully present the Mang Shen and the Earth Ox, together with the Spring-hill Throne, to their Imperial Majesties the Emperor, the Empress, and the Empress Dowager. The officials of the Metropolitan Prefecture and of these districts would raise them up so as to present them. The officials of the Ministry of Rites went before, with their President and Vice-presidents, while the Prefect and Vice-governor of the Metropolitan Prefecture followed behind. From Wu Men through the central gates they entered to Ch'ien Ch'ing Men (a gate almost in the center of the Forbidden City) and Tzǔ Ning Men (a gate in the far western section of the Palace), where they respectfully offered these objects. There the eunuch attendants received and handed them on to their Majesties. When the ceremony was completed, all retired, the Prefect of the Metropolitan Prefecture taking the Earth Ox away with him and beating it on all

---

[1] Mang Shen, otherwise known as Kou Mang 句 芒, was supposedly the son of the legendary Emperor Shao Hao 少 昊, who later became the tutelary spirit of spring. *Cf. Li Chi, op. cit.*, p. 250. According to whether this image is represented wearing shoes or barefoot, it is supposed that the coming season will be dry or wet, while varying colors painted on the ox likewise indicate varying types of weather.

sides so as to make a show thereby of encouraging agriculture. Floating banners and other small objects were carried in front as well.

> *Note*: This ceremony well indicates the great stress always placed on agriculture in China. It was hoped that the symbolic beating of the ox, used for plowing the fields, would induce a corresponding industry in cultivating the fields during the coming year. In later times, however, this original meaning has been lost, and the beating of the ox has been done simply to ward off pestilence.

During the Cheng T'ung period (1436-1449) of the Ming dynasty, the Metropolitan Prefecture each year at the Beginning of Spring had a Spring Ox and artificial spring flowers specially made, and brought these before the Emperor at the Palace of Virtue and Longevity (Jen Shou Kung), a total of three things in all.[1] For each of these, such materials as gold, silver, pearls, and chrysoprase were used at an expenditure of more than ninety thousand strings of cash. When Emperor Ching (1450-1456) ascended the throne, he decreed that the next year on the day of spring these three things should be still further elaborated, so that the local people of the district of Wan P'ing one after another made complaints saying that only flowers of the season should be used for these throughout. From this we may see that the Ming dynasty, when it encountered something which would give trouble to the people, was certainly not equal to the august frugality of the present dynasty.

LANTERN FESTIVAL (*Teng Chieh* 燈 節)

> *Note*: The Lantern Festival seems to have originated as an ancient ceremonial of welcoming the increasing light and warmth of the sun after the winter's cold, and so, though celebrated much earlier, may have certain analogies with our own Easter. It is also possible that it was originally a ceremony to induce rains for the spring planting.

The period from the thirteenth to the seventeenth is all called the Lantern Festival, but it is the fifteenth which is the true Lantern Festival. Each year on the day of the Lantern Festival there is a feast within the Palace, and fire-crackers are set off. While all shops display lanterns, it is those of the big streets, as at Tung Ssŭ P'ailou and Ti An Men, which are most numerous. The Ministry of Works

---

[1] Probably the Spring Ox, the Spring-hill Throne, and Mang Shen.

comes next, and after that the Ministry of War, and no other place can measure up to these.

Author's Note: In the ninth year of Kuang Hsü (1883) the lanterns at the Ministry of War were prohibited by Yen Wen-chieh.

As to Tung An Men, Hsin Chieh K'ou, and Hsi Ssŭ P'ailou, these places also in a lesser degree are worth looking at. There are variegated lanterns of every color, made from such materials as silk gauze, glass, and transparent horn, which are painted with scenes from old and new legends, thus adding to one's enjoyment. Ingenious merchants moreover make objects molded out of ice, and from young shoots of wheat, pattern figures of men and animals.[1] Decorative yet not extravagant, simple yet not coarse, these things are certainly worth viewing.

The fire-cracker shops manufacture fireworks of every variety, vying with each other in ingenuity and contending as to which shall be more original. There are such kinds as " small boxes," " flower pots," " fire and smoke poles " (i.e., rockets), " peonies strung on a thread," " lotus sprinkled with water," " golden plates " (i.e., pin-wheels), " falling moons," " grape arbors," " flags of fire," " double-kicking feet " (i.e., fire-crackers which explode once on the ground, and then again in the air), " ten explosions flying to heaven," " five devils noisily splitting apart," " eight-cornered rockets," " bombs for attacking the city of Hsiang Yang,"[2] and " lanterns of heaven and earth."

Wealthy and eminent households compete with one another in buying them, and the varicolored brilliance of " silver flowers " and " fire trees " dazzles the people. Carriages and horses raise a tremendous hubbub, while the sounds of playing and singing din the ears, lasting from daylight until the second drum (i.e., ten p.m.), when the smoke of fire-crackers and dust of feet gradually lessen. Then men's shadows fall stretched upon the ground, while in the

---

[1] Wooden frames in the form of the objects represented are covered with cotton on which wheat seeds have been laid. This is kept in a warm place and watered until the seeds send forth shoots. Such objects are rarely seen to-day.

[2] 襄 陽, a city on the Han River in Hupeh which has always occupied a very important strategic position.

heavens hangs the clear moon.[1]   Men, women, and children one by one begin to scatter to their homes with sounds of laughter.

The market sale of eatables and of dried and fresh fruits has been prepared for the celebration, with special stress on the *yüan hsiao* 元宵 (cakes specially eaten at this time), thus serving likewise to mark the advent of this festival.   There are also sellers of goldfish, which are kept in (many-sided) glass bowls, so that when one passes from side to side, the forms of the fish appear suddenly big or small— truly a feature to be found nowhere else.

According to the *Jih-hsia Chiu-wen-k'ao*,[2] during the Ming dynasty the lantern market was situated east of Tung Hua Men and Wang Fu Chieh, and west of Ch'ung Wen Chieh (better known as Hatamen Street), extending for about two *li*, with shops situated on both north and south.   This is to-day Lantern Market Street (Teng Shih K'ou). On market days all sorts of pearls and jades and precious things, as well as trifling things for daily use, were arranged, the stalls laid out in the street being crowded together, several rows facing each other, while all the upper storey buildings were equipped with rugs and mats as places for rest and refreshment.   The daily rent for one such building might be as much as several hundred strings of cash, and they all were intended for members of eminent families and their relatives.

As for lanterns, there were those of imitation pearls, silk gauze, transparent horn, stalks of wheat, and of *t'ung ts'ao*.[3]   For music there were wind, stringed, and other miscellaneous instruments.   As for fire-crackers, there were. . . . . [here follows another list of varieties]. The festival began on the eighth day and ended on the eighteenth, thus making a total of ten days and not the five days of the festival to-day.   The assemblage of various kinds of merchandise was at that time combined with the lanterns into a single fair at one spot, whereas

---

[1] Like so many Chinese festivals, the Lantern Festival comes at the time of full moon, since it falls on the fifteenth of the lunar month.

[2] This work, which is cited by our author more than any other, will hereafter be referred to as the *Jih-hsia*.

[3] 通草, i.e., *fatsia papyrifera*, a plant utilized to produce the rice paper used in the making of artificial flowers.

to-day lanterns are restricted to the Tartar City, while the fair (for other things) is restricted to Glazed Tile Factory (Liu Li Ch'ang).[1]

ENTERTAINMENT OF THE NINTH (*Yen Chiu* 莚 九)

The nineteenth day is called the *Yen Chiu*,[2] and each year on this day the Emperor goes to the feast and entertainment held at Small Gold Hall (Hsiao Chin Tien) at the Western Enclosure (Hsi Ch'ang Tzŭ),[3] where he witnesses games and wrestling bouts.[4] There the Mongolian princes and dukes (who have come to Peking on their yearly visit) wish him peace and announce their return (to Mongolia), while those officials who have the right to wear sable robes all discard them on this day and change to silver fox furs.

Note: During the Empire, it was only members of the nobility, and officials above a certain rank, who were granted such privileges as the wearing of sables, and no merchant, no matter how wealthy, was allowed to do so. The dates for changing from one type of clothing to another followed the calendar with inexorable exactitude, as is still the case in Japan to-day.

Among the common people there is nothing special to be recorded. But those who go to enjoy themselves at the White Cloud Temple (Po Yün Kuan) call this day the one of Meeting the Gods and Immortals (*Hui Shen Hsien* 會 神 仙)[5] . . . .

OPENING THE SEALS (*K'ai Yin* 開 印)[6]

The time when the seals (used in the government offices) are brought out, falls some time within the three-day period of the nineteenth, twentieth, and twenty-first. A propitious day and hour, notifications of which have been sent out in advance, are selected by the Imperial Board of Astronomy, for putting on Court robes and conducting the usual ceremonies. The administration of government follows this opening of the seals, (and the New Year holidays are now over).

---

[1] *Cf.* p. 17.

[2] That is to say, the ninth day in the *second* of the three ten-day periods in a month.

[3] The Hsiao Chin Tien is a popular name for the Tzŭ Kuang Ko (Throne hall of Purple Effulgence), a building on the west bank of the Central Lake or Chung Hai, where the Emperor used to receive in audience Mongol envoys and tributary princes. Here too was the place where the first general audience for western diplomatic representatives was held in 1873. The name Gold Hall (Chin Tien) is a literary term for the Imperial palace, so that the term Hsiao Chin Tien means Little Palace, perhaps with reference to the fact that the Emperor only received barbarians here.

[4] For a detailed account of such a feast at Jehol, translated from Chinese records, see SVEN HEDIN, *Jehol, City of Emperors*, pp. 171-173, London, 1932.

[5] On this, *cf.* p. 14.

[6] *Cf.* also the putting away of the seals before New Year, p. 95.

DEVIL DANCES, OR 'BEATING OF THE DEVILS' (*Ta Kuei* 打 鬼)

The beating of the devils was originally a Buddhist practice of the western border-lands, and has nothing particularly strange about it. It is the same as the custom coming down from olden times of the exorcism of evil spirits at the nine gates (of the Capital). Each year at the time of the Devil Beating, the Lama priests all dress themselves up as deities of Heaven, so as to drive out the evil devils. So many are the people of the Capital who go to look on, that it appears as if ten thousand families had deserted the streets. Being favorably inclined to Buddhist practices, the Court especially delegates one of the Junior Assistant-Chamberlains of the Imperial Bodyguard to witness the ceremony—indeed the idea of the Sage " putting on his Court robes and standing on the eastern steps." [1] The time for the Devil Beating at the Yellow Temple (Huang Ssŭ) comes on the fifteenth day [2]; at the Black Temple (Hei Ssŭ) on the twenty-third ; and at the Lama Temple (Yung Ho Kung) on the thirtieth.

According to the *Ch'en-yüan Shih-lüeh*, the eastern part of the Yellow Temple lies outside An Ting Men, where there is a drill-ground of the Bordered Yellow Banner. [3] In the eighth year of Shun Chih (1651) it was erected in accordance with Imperial order on the foundation of the old Monastery of Universal Peace (P'u Ching Ch'an Ssŭ), while in the twenty-third year of K'ang Hsi (1684) it was repaired. West of the temple is a gate of glazed tile called the Wall of Pure Metamorphosis (Ch'ing Ching Hua Ch'eng). Behind are two stone monuments, a stone platform, and a stone stupa eighty feet high which is carved with exquisite workmanship (with scenes from Buddha's life). On top is a golden umbrella-like cover, the brilliance of which dazzles the eye. This is traditionally called the Pan-ch'an Lama Stupa, he also being called the Pock-marked (*Pan-chen* 瘢 疹)

---

[1] This has reference to what the *Lun Yü*, X, 10, says of Confucius that "when his fellow-villagers held a procession to expel the pestilential influences, he put on his Court robes and stood on the eastern steps " so as to show his respect for local custom.

[2] This is now no longer held.

[3] The Manchu military organization was composed of eight divisions or Banners : the Plain Yellow, White, Red, and Blue Banners, and the Bordered Banners of the same colors. These troops consisted of Manchus, Mongols, and Chinese.

Lama, probably because he here contracted and died of smallpox, and this tower indicates his place of rest.[1]

At the sides are four banners bearing holy texts written in the forty-eighth year of Ch'ien Lung (1783) by P'eng Yüan-jui (who was then President of the Ministry of Works). The Imperial inscription of the Wall of Pure Metamorphosis is east of the platform, and is written in four languages : Manchu, Chinese, Mongolian, and Sanskrit. Behind the pagoda is a building called the Hall of Wisdom and Fragrance (Hui Hsiang Ko).

The Lama Temple, or Yung Ho Kung, is inside Tung Chih Men about a *li* directly north of Pei Hsin Ch'iao. Before he became Emperor, it was the palace of Shih Tsung Hsien Huang Ti (usually known under his reign title as Yung Cheng, 1723-1735), who after ascending the throne ordered it to be called the Palace of Concord and Harmony (Yung Ho Kung).[2]

The Black Temple is outside Te Sheng Men about three *li* to the north-west. . . . . That a Lama temple should have been called Black Temple was probably with reference to some iron-coloured glazed tiles, but these are now no longer in existence. Its posterior temple has an iron incense pavilion which was built in the *Yi-mao* year of K'ang Hsi (1675).

Filling the Granary (*T'ien Ts'ang* 填倉)

Each year on the twenty-fifth day grain and rice merchants go to sacrifice to the Granary God (Ts'ang Shen 倉 神), when there are many fire-crackers. Not all householders take part in this sacrifice, but nevertheless they must boil something to drink and eat with which to reward their house servants. This is called " filling the granary."

According to what the *Pei-ching Sui-hua-chi* says, people and families on the twenty-fifth day would buy pork, beef, and mutton to be freely feasted on during the entire day, and if a guest should

---

[1] The Pan-ch'an Lamas are believed to be successive incarnations of Amitābha Buddha, and head the great Tashi-lhunpo Monastery in Tibet, with power seccond only to that of the Dalai Lamas, who head the Yellow Sect. This pagoda was erected in 1781 as a memorial to the Pan-ch'an Lama who died there.

[2] It was then converted into a temple in accord with the ancient custom that the palace of a prince who became Emperor could not be inhabited by his descendants.

come, he was required to remain, and had to eat to repletion before going. And this was called "filling the granary."

Note: Here is an example of sympathetic magic. Filling the human stomach will induce the Granary God to fill the granaries.

What this paragraph records is in a general way the same as the present custom. But to-day it is only the rich and noble families who follow it, and there is no one who eats beef, nor is there any talk of guests being forced to remain. What has here been recorded is evidently only a one-sided account.

BIG BELL TEMPLE (*Ta Chung Ssŭ* 大 鐘 寺)

The Big Bell Temple was originally the Temple of Awakening to a Sense of Former Existence (Chüeh Sheng Ssŭ), and has derived its present name from its big bell. It is the spot where during the year may take place the ceremony of asking for rain.[1] Each year, beginning from the first day of the first month, the temple is opened for ten days, when sightseers assemble, men and women coming in groups like clouds. Many of the young people of the Capital enjoy themselves at this time by racing in carts or on horses. They stir up dust and rush about like lightning, tiring themselves out without stopping. The expense for one mount may be as much as several hundred taels. Is this not indeed a long surviving tradition of the fine horse fairs of Peking?[2]

According to the *Jih-hsia*, this Hua Yen[3] bell was cast in the Ming dynasty during the Yung Lo period (1403-1424). It is fifteen feet high and fourteen feet in diameter. The knob (on top of the bell, by which it is suspended), is seven feet high, and the thickness

---

[1] This ceremony is usually performed by farmers who assemble in impressive groups, wearing willow wreaths (the willow is associated with water), to pray to the Dragon King (Lung Wang 龍 王), who has control over rain. In former times prayers for rain were conducted at the Big Bell Temple by the Emperor himself.

[2] For other horse races, *cf.* pp. 49 and 69. These races were very colorful affairs, and used to attract large crowds, but have all been given up now. Many officials and Manchus of noble blood used to attend them in their gorgeous costumes. They were pacing, rather than galloping races, and the women often used to have their own fun by racing in Peking carts!

[3] 華 嚴, a Buddhist sect which was important during the T'ang dynasty (618-906) but is now of little significance.

of the bell is seven inches. It weighs eighty-seven thousand catties (one hundred and sixteen thousand pounds). The entire Fa Hua Sūtra [1] is engraved in the " model " (*k'ai* 楷) style of characters both inside and outside. The characters are each one half inch in size, and close together like the teeth of a comb. They were written by the scholar Shen Tu, (a noted calligrapher who was Sub-chancellor of the Grand-secretariat under Yung Lo).

During the Chia Ching period (1522-1566) the bell was suspended in Wan Shou Ssŭ.[2] But someone spoke about it later on, saying that it was not proper for the sound of metal to be heard in the white tiger quarter of the Capital. Thereupon its tower was done away with and the bell was buried in the ground.[3]

During the present dynasty, in the eighth year of Ch'ien Lung (1743), the bell was moved and set up in the Chüeh Sheng Ssŭ, now known as the Big Bell Temple, which lies seven *li* outside Te Sheng Men [4] at Tseng Chia Chuang, north-west of the Earth Wall.[5] In the eleventh year of Yung Cheng (1733) the bell tower was constructed, fifty feet in height. It is square below and round above, and there are windows on all four sides. At the rear is a circular staircase which ascends on the left and descends on the right, while the bell hangs in the center. Its entire mass is of pure bronze, exactly upright, and with a fine sheen. It is in truth of extreme preciousness! Alas that I have never yet once heard it sound! In the front hall is a stone

---

[1] 法 華 經, a translation of the Sadharmapundarika Sūtra, made by the famous Indian monk Kumarajiva, some time after his arrival in China in A.D. 401. It is one of the most important and profound of the Buddhist scriptures, and is about as long as the Four Gospels and the Acts of the Apostles.

[2] Concerning this temple, *cf.* pp. 36-37.

[3] The quarter of the white tiger signifies the west, for, according to Chinese cosmology, the white tiger symbolizes the west, the green dragon the east, the scarlet bird the south, and the black warrior or black tortoise the north. It is hard to understand why the sound of metal should be deemed unpropitious for the west, for according to the cosmology of the Chinese five elements, metal is just that element which corresponds to the west. The idea seems to be that the sound of metal in the west might have a disturbing effect upon the eastern quarter (the quarter of the element wood), since metal is supposed to overcome wood. But if removed to the Big Bell Temple north of the Capital, the bell would be harmless because the north is the quarter of water, and the element metal is supposed to produce the element water. This also may be the reason why it was at this temple that prayers for rain were held.

[4] More easily reached to-day, however, from Hsi Chih Men, the north gate in the west city wall.

[5] The still surviving earth rampart north of Peking, which formed the wall of Peking (then Cambaluc) during the Yüan dynasty (1280-1368).

tablet of the twelfth year of Yung Cheng (1734) with an inscription composed by Chang Jo-ai of the Hanlin Academy.[1]

TEMPLE OF THE WHITE CLOUDS (*Po Yün Kuan* 白 雲 觀)

The Po Yün Kuan is five or six *li* south-west outside Fou Ch'eng Men.[2] Its origin is very early, for it has existed ever since the Chin (1115-1234) and Yüan (1280-1367) dynasties. The four characters inside the temple, 萬 古 長 春 *Wan ku ch'ang ch'un*, (which may be translated as "ten thousand ages of eternal spring") are still traditionally held to have been written by Ch'iu Ch'ang-ch'un (founder of the temple).

Each year, beginning from the first day of the first month, the temple is thrown open for nineteen days, when sightseers come continuously and carriages and horses rush about. On the nineteenth day it is even more busy, this day being called that of Meeting the Gods and Immortals (*Hui Shen Hsien* 會 神 仙).[3] It is traditionally said that on the night of the eighteenth day there will be a descent of the Immortal Perfect One,[4] who will transform himself perhaps into a pilgrim, perhaps into a beggar. Those who by some chance should then encounter him, will thereby ward off illness and prolong their years. Therefore there are always from three to five Taoist priests sitting cross-legged in a group below the corridors with the hope of experiencing just one meeting. But after all I know not whether they actually have such a meeting or not!

Inside the temple is an Old Men's Hall where all the old Taoist priests live. Though these, to be sure, are not divine immortals, yet ever among them are a few more than a hundred years old, which is evident proof of their self-discipline and training. Behind the temple are a pavilion and a garden. These have been constructed in recent years and were formerly not there.

---

[1] Literally, the "Forest of Pens," the academy of scholars who reached the highest honors under the Imperial examination system.

[2] I.e., P'ing Tse Men, the south gate in the west city wall. The temple is more easily reached, however, from Hsi Pien Men, which is the gate at the north-west corner of the Chinese city.

[3] *Cf.* p. 9.

[4] A Taoist term for those who through special meditation, diet, breathing exercises, etc., have obtained immortality and supernatural powers.

According to the *Jih-hsia*, the Po Yün Kuan is on the site of the old ruins of the Palace of the Great Ultimate (T'ai Chi Kung). Inside is a sculptured clay image of Ch'iu, the Perfect One, with a white face from which whiskers and eyebrows are absent (so as to give him an appearance of eternal youth). On the nineteenth day of the first month the people of the Capital come to offer sacrifice, this being called the *Yen Chiu* 燕 九 festival.

The Perfect One (i.e., Ch'iu Ch'ang-ch'un) was a native of Ch'i-hsia in Teng-chou. [1] His first name was Ch'u-chi 處機, and his fancy name or pseudonym (*hao* 號) was Ch'ang-ch'un 長春. When the Master (i.e., Ch'iu Ch'ang-ch'un) was nineteen years old, he studied the doctrines of the sect of Complete Truth (*Ch'üan Chen* 全真) at the K'un Lun Mountains in Ning Hai. [2] In the *Chi-mao* year (1219), Yüan T'ai Tsu (Genghis Khan) sent an envoy from the country of the Nai-mans [3] to summon him, but even before the envoy had arrived, the Perfect One spoke to his disciples, saying : " Pack up quickly ! The celestial (i.e., Imperial) envoy is summoning me, and I must go." Next day, when the envoy did arrive, the Master departed together with eighteen disciples. They passed through several tens of countries and traversed more than ten thousand *li* before arriving at the Snow Mountains. [4]

Genghis Khan was at that time engaged in his western campaigns and each day there was fighting. The Perfect One, each time he spoke, would say that the person who wishes to make the world one, should not delight in killing men. When asked how to govern, he said that what was fundamental was to reverence Heaven and love the people. And on being asked the method for prolonging life and remaining a long time in this world, he replied that what was important was to purify the heart and lessen the desires. Genghis Khan was greatly pleased, and ordered the Historian of the Left to make a record of what was said.

[1] 棲 霞 in 登 州, east of the present district of Tan in Shantung.

[2] 宵 海, in Shantung, not in Chinese Turkestan.

[3] 奈 曼, in Chinese Turkestan. See Vladimirtsov, *The Life of Chingis-Khan*, London, 1930, pp. 57-61.

[4] *Hsüeh Shan* 雪 山. Identified as the Hindu Kush by Arthur Waley in his *The Travels of an Alchemist*, London, 1931, p. 96.

After the Perfect One returned to the east, he was given the title of Divine Immortal (*Shen Hsien* 神 仙), and authorized to be the Great Sect Master (*Ta Tsung Shih* 大 宗 師), in charge of the Taoist religion over the entire world. He was told to dwell in Yen (an old name for Peking), in the Palace of the Great Ultimate, which was later changed to be that of the Palace of Eternal Spring (Ch'ang Ch'un Kung), and is the present Po Yün Kuan. At the age of eighty the Perfect One left his corporeal frame and departed as an Immortal.

Note : It is from this time that Taoism has been divided into the Northern School, which has its headquarters at Po Yün Kuan, and which stresses meditation and philosophical speculation ; and the Southern School, which has its headquarters on the Dragon and Tiger Mountain (Lung Hu Shan) in Kiangsi, ruled by the hereditary " Taoist Popes " of the Chang family, and which stresses exorcism, charm magic, and elixirs.

TEMPLE OF THE EUNUCH TS'AO (*Ts'ao Lao Kung Kuan* 曹 老 公 觀)

The Ts'ao Lao Kung Kuan is inside Hsi Chih Men on the north side of the street. Each year, beginning from the first day of the first month, the temple is opened for half a month, when there are many pilgrims. But the halls have collapsed, the walls are not intact, and the ancient Buddhas have fallen down. Certainly there is nothing special to be seen. There do exist two stone tablets, the left of which has been inscribed with seven maxims in two sections by Ch'ien Lung, while the right one is without writing. Behind the hall is a round incense burner which was made in the *Hsin-mao* year of Ming Wan Li (1591). The central hall has a square iron incense burner which was made in the ninth year of Ch'ung Cheng (1636) by the eunuch, Sun Chi-wu, Commander of the Cavalry, and others.

According to the *Jih-hsia*, the temple was named the Temple of Exalted Origin (Ch'ung Yüan Kuan), and was founded by the Ming dynasty eunuch, Ts'ao Hua-shun. It was repaired in the twenty-third year of Ch'ien Lung (1758), thus making its appearance once more firm and beautiful, and its Buddhist images strong and awe-inspiring. But in the hundred odd years since that time it has completely collapsed, and there has been no restoration of the old temple. Some say that when Ts'ao Hua-shun erected it, he stored some gold in a vault within the temple in anticipation of future repairs, and therefore Peking has a saying about it : " Seven paces from the inside, and seven paces from the outside : There the temple will fall, and there the temple will be repaired." [1] But after all there is no evidence of the truth of these words.

Note : This temple is now no longer in existence, and its site is occupied by Northeastern University.

FAIR AT 'GLAZED TILE FACTORY' (Liu Li Ch'ang 琉璃廠)

The Leased Enclosure (Ch'ang Tien) is about two li outside Cheng Yang Men (i.e., Ch'ien Men).[2] Of old it was called the Village of the Sea King (Hai Wang Ts'un), which is the same as the present Liu Li Ch'ang (Glazed Tile Factory, once operated here by) the Ministry of Works. Shops stand like a forest along both the north and south sides of a street about two li long. They deal especially in curios, calligraphy and paintings, paper, books, and stone rubbings, so that this is a place indeed where the man of letters may look around and enjoy himself. Beginning from the first day of the first month, there is a fair here lasting half a month. Children's toys are to be found at the Leased Enclosure,[3] whereas jewelry is to be found in the Temple of the God of Fire (Huo Shen Miao), where pearls, precious stones, crystal, jade, and bronze vessels are on display. Daily there are long lines of carriages of rich and noble people who come hoping to obtain some unique rarity.

Among precious stones, green jade is most esteemed, so that the price of a single archery ring [4] or a tube to hold one's Mandarin hat feather may cost as much as ten thousand taels. Besides green jade, snuff bottles made of colored glass are also greatly esteemed, only they must be of the Imperial kilns. The snuff bottles of the Ku Yüeh Hsüan 古月軒 hall-mark are of the finest quality, while the modern products are not worth being mentioned.

---

[1] I.e., the treasure is buried at a central spot seven paces equidistant from the inner and outer walls. The original reads :

Li ch'i pu, wai ch'i pu; 裏七步，外七步;
Kuan-er tao, kuan-er hsiu. 觀兒倒，觀兒偹.

[2] It is now more readily reached, however, through Ho P'ing Men, a gate west of Ch'ien Men, which was opened in the wall in 1925.

[3] The place where the tile kilns once stood, and so named because it was later leased to curio dealers.

[4] A ring put on the thumb to prevent it from being cut by the taut bow string.

It seems that the taste for luxuries has differed during different periods. Thus during the Ch'ien Lung period (1736-1795) coral was especially esteemed, while garnet was little cared for, whereas later on garnet was again valued, and more recently green jade has again been still more favorably regarded, together with snuff bottles made of colored glass. Among literary men there are also those who esteem old jade (i.e., jade of a type similar to that buried in early times with the dead), such as that of flute mouthpieces and sword trimmings. Their ancient tints are innumerable, and it is difficult indeed to decide which is genuine and which is false. Therefore I have often said: " If inanimate things could only speak, we should avoid a great deal of argument as to their authenticity." As to old porcelain, it is extremely scarce, for much of it has already been bought and taken away by foreigners.

According to the *Jih-hsia*, east of Liu Li Ch'ang lies the grave of Li Nei-cheng, a Provincial Censor of the Liao dynasty (907-1124), the stone inscription of which was found in the ground in the thirty-sixth year of Ch'ien Lung (1771) by Meng Hao, Director of the Ministry of Works. On this inscription it is stated that the burial had taken place in the Village of the Sea King (Hai Wang Ts'un). [1]

EAST AND WEST TEMPLES

The west temple is called Protect the Country Temple (Hu Kuo Ssŭ), and is north-west of the Imperial City, directly west of Ting Fu Ta Chieh. The east temple is called Temple of Prosperity and Happiness (Lung Fu Ssŭ), and is west of Tung Ssŭ P'ailou, and directly north of the Horse Market (Ma Shih). Beginning with the first month, the western temple is opened every seven and eight days, and the eastern temple every nine and ten days. [2] On the days when the

---

[1] So called because about A.D. 977 there was a man here who set himself up as contractor for the boats used to convey grain across the numerous creeks then in this region, and who was named the Sea King owing to his extortions.

[2] That is, the west temple is open on the seventh, eighth, seventeenth, eighteenth, twenty-seventh, and twenty-eighth days of each month, while the east temple is open on the ninth, tenth, nineteenth, twentieth, twenty-ninth, and thirtieth. Since this time, however, Lung Fu Ssŭ has added the two-day periods of the eleventh and twelfth, twenty-first and twenty-second, and first and second, while still a third fair is now held at the White Stupa Temple (Pai T'a Ssŭ) inside P'ing Tse Men, on the fifth, sixth, fifteenth, sixteenth, twenty-fifth, and twenty-sixth days. These dates, and the dates of all other temples having monthly fairs, now follow the Western calendar.

temples are open there is an assembly of goods of every description. Everything is to be had here, including all varieties of pearls and jades, silks, clothing, things to eat and drink, curios, calligraphy and paintings, flowers and birds, insects and fish, and objects of daily use, as well as fortune tellers, and miscellaneous entertainers. These are the two great fairs of the Capital.

The flower stands of the two temples are especially fine to look at. In spring time it is the fruit trees which are most numerous ; in summer it is the jasmines ; in autumn it is the *kuei chü* 桂菊 (*osmanthus fragrans*, a small clustering white or yellow flower) ; and in winter it is the narcissus. As to spring flowers, such as the peony, begonia, lilac, and peach, these are all made to blossom during the severe winter. Their rare beauty is remarkable, and by means of the skill (which it exhibits) is quite worthy to hold for itself (the fruits of) Heaven's labors. (The men who cultivate these flowers) have here stolen a march on the *Yüeh Ling*,[1] and have delved deeply in their investigations into the principles of things.[2] Alas that none have produced books on the subject !

In western books on agriculture I have seen the statement that from the produce of one grain kernel, one hundred thousand kernels may be obtained. If with the methods used in rearing these flowers one were to raise such (a kernel, the number of kernels produced) would certainly far surpass this number. But human labor is costly, and the question of irrigation is also difficult. Such means are feasible for the production of luxuries, but certainly not for that of ordinary crops. Thus it would be quite possible to make such things as squashes, cucumbers, egg-plant, and string-beans all ripen during the severe winter, and their colors and tastes would all be excellent. But the cost would be too high, and hence they could not be food for everyone, which is certainly a clear evidence of the impracticability of the idea.

---

[1] This is one of the oldest of Chinese almanacs, and now forms one of the chapters in the *Li Chi*. Cf. *Sacred Books of the East*, XXVII, 249-310. It gives frequent warning against the natural disasters which will overtake anyone who follows at any one season the rules pertaining to another season. Hence the reference here, with respect to spring flowers made to bloom in winter.

[2] This phrase is reminiscent of a famous sentence occurring in the first section of the *Ta Hsüeh* (Great Learning) : " The extension of knowledge lies in the investigation of things."

According to the *Jih-hsia*, Hu Kuo Ssü. . . . . is the former dwelling of T'o T'o, who was Prime Minister during the Yüan dynasty (in the Chih Cheng period, 1341-1367). Inside the temple is a Hall of the Thousand Buddhas at the side of which once stood figures of an old bearded man, wearing a bonnet and red clothing, and an old woman in a red dress with head-dress. These were the images of him (T'o T'o) and his wife, but are now no longer in existence.

Lung Fu Ssŭ was established during the Ming dynasty in the fourth year of Ching T'ai (1453), with the toil of ten thousand laborers. Inside the temple is a platform-balustrade of white stone, which is an antiquity from the Hall of the Soaring Phœnix (Hsiang Feng Tien) from within the southern (part of the palace) of Emperor Ying Tsung, (who reigned 1436-1449, was captured by Mongols, and then reigned again 1457-1464). During the present dynasty in the first year of Yung Cheng (1723), the temple was repaired and added to, and has a stone tablet with words by Emperor Shih Tsung (i.e., Yung Cheng). In comparison with Hu Kuo Ssŭ it has remained better preserved.

> *Author's Note* : On the twenty-second day of the tenth month of the twenty-seventh year of Kuang Hsü (December 3, 1901), Lung Fu Ssŭ was burned down.

TEMPLE OF THE GOD OF THE SOIL (*T'u Ti Miao* 土 地 廟)

> *Note :* These local tutelary divinities of the soil are probably among China's oldest gods. Each one presides over a district roughly circular in shape, and about ten *li* in radius, except in cities, where their area of jurisdiction is greatly restricted. The shrine is situated in the center of such a district, usually near a road, and is of the utmost simplicity : a roofed altar open in front and containing images of the God of the Soil and his wife.

The T'u Ti Miao lies outside Hsüan Wu Men on the west side of T'u Ti Hsieh Chieh. Beginning with the first month, there is a temple fair on the third, thirteenth, and twenty-third days of each month.[1] There are no valuable things, but only a flower display and pigeon market, with little else to be seen.

According to the *Jih-hsia*, the founding of the T'u Ti Miao was very early. There is a stone tablet of the forty-third year of Wan Li (1615) which says with reference to it : " The Hall of the

---

[1] The second, twelfth, and twenty-second days have now been added.

Ancient Traces of the Old Ruler [1] (Ku Chi Lao Chün T'ang 古蹟 老君堂) is now the T'u Ti Miao of the Capital." During Liao (907-1124) and Chin (1115-1234) times the temple was outside the east gate of the Capital, but at present there is no way of finding out its exact location.

FLOWER MARKET (*Hua-er Shih* 花兒市)

Flower Market is outside Ch'ung Wen Men (i.e., Hatamen gate) extending eastward. Beginning with the first month, there is a fair on the fourth, fourteenth, and twenty-fourth days of each month, the objects sold being all things for everyday use. It is called Flower Market, not with reference to natural flowers of the season, but rather to the paper flowers which women stick in their hair. Among the flowers are those of *t'ung ts'ao*, silk gauze, and. . . . . [here follow technical names of two other varieties], which look very much like the real ones indeed. In addition to the Flower Market, there is a pigeon market, which is in a small alley north of the shops.

Note: It was also near here that pigeons were reared for the express purpose of stealing grain from the Imperial granaries. They were taught to fly there, eat their fill, and return, whereupon they would be forced to retch up the contents of their crop. It is estimated that a flock of one hundred pigeons could thus collect fifty pounds of grain a day for its owner. *Cf.* Arlington and Lewisohn, *In Search of Old Peking*, pp. 227 f.

According to the *Chü-i-lu*, the Flower Market of the Capital sells two kinds of yellow pigeons, whose plumage is the color of gold, and the price of which is extremely high, etc. Indeed there are many Pekinese who delight in rearing pigeons, the varieties of which are extremely numerous. Thus among the ordinary kinds are such varieties as " dotted," " jade winged," " phœnix-headed white," " two-headed black," " small ash-black," " purple sauce," " snow flowers," " silver tailed," " four-piece jade," " magpie flowers," " heel and head," " flowery necked," and " Taoist priest hat." And among the valuable varieties are such as " short-beaked white," " egret white," " black ox," " iron ox," " azure plumage," " crane's elegance," " toad-eyed grey," " wild duck of the Great Dipper," " bronze back," " mottled back," " silver back," " square-edged

[1] The Old Ruler (Lao Chün) is a term referring to the Taoist sage, Lao Tzŭ.

unicorn," " striped sandals," " cloud plate," " blue plate," " parrot-beak white," " parrot-beak spotted," " purple black," " purple dotted," " purple jade wings," " black head, " iron winged," and " jade circlet."

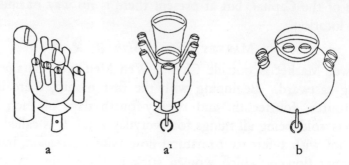

a   a¹   b

PIGEON WHISTLES

(a, a¹) *Shao-tzŭ* (side and front view). (b) *Hu-lu*. The drawings are one-half actual size. The whistles are made of bamboo and weigh 10 grams. They are attached above the tail of the bird by the metal ring.

Whenever the pigeons are let out to fly, bamboo whistles should be attached to their tails. These are called *hu-lu* 壺盧 and are also called whistles (*shao-tzŭ* 哨子). The *hu-lu* are divided into those which are large and small, whereas of the *shao-tzu*, there are those of three pipes attached together, of five, of thirteen, of eleven, double ones, ones with obstructed openings, and ones of many small tubes surrounding one large one. When the pigeons wheel overhead, their sound rises even to the clouds, containing within it all five notes (of the Chinese scale). Truly it gives joy, and a release to the emotions! As to what people of former times called " framework pigeons " (*chia ko* 架鴿), these no longer exist to-day.[1]

Again, the *Yü-shih Pien-lin* says that in the first month of spring many boys and girls of the Capital would cut out colored materials to make flowers and grasshoppers, and put them on their heads. This is to-day called " noisy clamor " (*nao jang-jang* 鬧嚷嚷), and is the same as what of old was called " noisy adornment " (*nao chuang* 鬧裝 i.e., gay or holiday adornment). And are not the silk flowers thus a source of childish amusement ?

[1] This term is not clear. Mr. Ono Katsutoshi (see Introduction p. xvi) in his Japanese translation (p. 70, Note 6) suggests (without giving documentation) that this puzzling term refers to pigeons carried on a stick ('framework') on which they perch and to which they are tied.

TEMPLES TO THE GOD OF MEDICINE (*Yao Wang Miao* 藥 王 廟)

The Small Temple of the God of Medicine is inside Tung Chih Men on the north side of the street. The North Temple of the God of Medicine is on the Former Drum Tower Avenue (Chiu Ku Lou Ta Chieh). Beginning with the first month, there is a temple fair on the first and fifteenth days of each month, at which all sorts of things especially used by women are sold, but there is not a great deal to be witnessed.

Note: The North Temple is now in complete ruins, while the fairs at both temples have been abandoned.

TRAINED MICE, MONKEYS, PUPPETS, AND ' BOATS THAT RUN ON LAND '

Those who train mice have a wooden box, to the top of which is attached a horizontal framework, and when their mice are well-trained they can do such tricks as drawing up water (as if from a well) and running through hoops, all of which begin and stop to the sound of a gong. Those with trained monkeys have a plumed or black crêpe bonnet concealed inside a wooden box. This the monkey takes out of the box with his paw, puts on, and then sits down with the dignified aspect of officials sitting in a row in court, while the monkey man sings a rude ditty with rising and falling modulations. Certainly the ancient reference to " the monkey wearing a cap " applies here.[1] Moreover, the monkey can plow and ride horseback, all through obeying the directions of his master. When plowing, a dog takes the place of the ox. When riding, a sheep replaces the horse.

PUPPET SHOW

---

[1] This term, *mu hou erh kuan* 沐 猴 而 冠, occurs in the *Shih Chi* (Historical Records), Chap. 7 (*cf.* Chavannes, *Mémoires historiques de Sse-ma Ts'ien*, II, 283), and refers to a mean and ordinary person who has the airs and manners of a monkey.

Marionettes or puppets are operated by a man inside a cloth tent, above whose head is a small platform. While he sings he presents " Beating the Tiger," " Racing Horses," and other miscellaneous

'BOAT THAT RUNS ON LAND'

pieces. The "boat that runs on land" consists of village boys dressed up as girls, who hold in their hands a cloth boat (with which they move about), singing a rude ditty the while. The idea is to represent someone who is gathering lotus while floating upon a lake. But how is it that they do not see their own crudeness?

All these various entertainments are given by peasants from the south of the Capital, and are most common during the first month. But when the busy time for farming comes, these people abandon their arts and return to their tilling.

CHAPTER II—THE SECOND MONTH

Sun Cakes (*T'ai Yang Kao* 太陽糕)

On the first day of the second month merchants make small cakes out of rice flour which cost five coppers a layer. The image of a small chicken, a little over an inch in size, is put on top, and these are called sun cakes. When people of the Capital sacrifice to the sun, they buy three to five of these and offer them.

Note: A rooster is supposed by the Chinese to inhabit the sun, hence the effigy put on the cakes.

Dragon Raising His Head (*Lung T'ai T'ou* 龍抬頭)

The second day of the second month is the ancient festival of Middle Harmony (*Chung Ho* 中和, so called because it comes in the middle of spring), while the people of to-day call it the time when the dragon raises his head.[1] The cakes eaten on this day are called dragon-scale cakes (*lung lin ping* 龍鱗餅), and the noodles that are eaten are called dragon-whisker noodles (*lung hsü mien* 龍鬚麵). In the women's quarters needlework is stopped for fear that they might injure the dragon's eyes.

Spring Equinox (*Ch'un Fen* 春分)

Before and after the spring equinox the various official temples (i.e., those of the God of War, of the God of the Soil, of the God of the City, etc.) all have great officials coming to them to offer sacrifice. Members of noble families also sacrifice on this day to their ancestors, and at the autumn equinox they do likewise.

According to what the *Yüeh-ling Kuang-i* says, the word " division " (*fen*, in the term *ch'un fen*) means half. It is the half of ninety days, but with respect to the summer and winter seasons this term " division " is not used. Between Heaven and Earth there are but two fluids.[2]

---

[1] It is then, supposedly, that the Great Dragon, Ruler of the Empire of Worms, calls forth the insects from the cocoons in which they have been resting during the winter.

[2] The *yang* 陽 and the *yin* 陰 are the male and female fluids, the interactions of which are supposed to produce all natural phenomena.

The *yang* is born in the *tzŭ* (eleventh month, i.e., after the winter solstice, when the days again become longer), and reaches its apogee in the *wu* (fifth month, i.e., at the summer solstice). This " division " falls in the middle between these two times.

Author's Note : From the Beginning of Spring (*Li Ch'un*) to the Beginning of Summer (*Li Hsia*) is a period of ninety days.

Festival of ' Pure Brightness ' (*Ch'ing Ming* 清 明)

The *Ch'ing Ming* is the same as the Cold Food Festival (*Han Shih* 寒 食),[1] which is also called the Festival of Prohibited Smoke (*Chin Yen Chieh* 禁 烟 節).

Note : The traditional explanation for the origin of the Cold Food Festival is that Duke Wen of the State of Chin, when he became duke of his state in 635 B.C. after many years spent in wandering through the other feudal states of the China of his time, rewarded many of those who had accompanied him. One of them, Chieh Tzŭ-t'ui, who once in a time of famine had cut off a piece of his own arm to give to the Duke as food, was inadvertently overlooked. Filled with disappointment, Chieh thereupon retired to a forest, where he was burned to death when Duke Wen, in his endeavors to make him come forth, set fire to the forest. The Duke, filled with remorse, decreed that from that time onward no fires should be lighted on that day. But the accounts in the *Tso Chuan* (Legge, *Chinese Classics*, V, 191 f.) and the *Shih Chi* (Chavannes, *Mémoires historiques de Sse-ma Ts'ien*, IV, 296) make no mention of this burning, and the whole explanation sounds like a rationalization of the ancient practice, found in many parts of the world, of marking the interval between the yearly extinction of the old fire and the lighting of the new.

People of old greatly stressed it, whereas the people of to-day do not make a festival of it, so that children, carrying willows, simply offer sacrifices to, and sweep the graves of, their ancestors. Those of noble families who sacrifice and sweep, make, in addition to the ordinary sacrificial utensils, pennons and parasols out of colored paper money (such as is burned for the dead), which are laid out on the left of the grave. When the sacrifice is finished, the descendants take these with their own hands outside the grave gate and burn them, and these are called *fo-to* 佛 多.[2] But the common people do not have this custom.

---

[1] Our author is in error here, for the Cold Food Festival actually precedes the *Ch'ing Ming* by one day, which in its turn, being based on the solar calendar, usually falls around April 5.

[2] A Manchu term which refers specifically to the willow branches which are set upright during the Shamanist rites practised to secure happiness.

According to what the *Hsi-ching-chih* says, the *Ch'ing Ming* was much stressed in the customs of the Liao dynasty (907-1124). On that day everybody, from those in the Palace and the officials down to the common people, amused themselves by swinging on swings. But from the Ming dynasty (1368-1644) onward, this custom has long been changed, and there has been no revival of this sport of being " half an Immortal." [1]

Again, according to what the *Sui-shih Pai-wen* says, the various creatures are now growing and it is a time of purity and brightness, and is therefore called the Pure Brightness (*Ch'ing Ming*). As to the wearing of willow wreaths on *Ch'ing Ming*, this goes back to Kao Tsung of the T'ang dynasty (reigned 650-683), who once when wearing short clothing and buskins while at Wei-yang,[2] gave to each of his assembled officers a willow circlet, saying that by wearing them they might avoid scorpion poison. What is done to-day seems to be a survival of this old idea.

Note :   This also is probably a rationalization. The willow, with its hardiness and its tender green leaves, is an emblem of vitality, and hence a talisman against evil spirits. Also, as we have seen (Note on p. 12), it is a powerful rain charm, perhaps because it so often grows near water. The *Ch'ing Ming* itself was probably originally a festival marking the renewal of life in spring and the time of mating, and hence similar in certain ways to our own May Day festival. From this it gradually changed, by a not unnatural process, to a festival for the care of the dead, who from the next world protect the living.

SALE OF SPRING CHICKENS AND DUCKS

During the last decade (twenty-first to twenty-ninth or thirtieth) of the second month comes the sale of young ducks and chickens. Then the cries of the vendors resound along the streets and business is brisk, the prosperity of the Capital being shown by the fact that several ten thousands of chickens and ducks are sold each day. These are all incubated through human effort, and do not hatch by themselves. The places which engage in this business are called chicken and duck houses, and are found in the Ch'i Hua Men and Tung Chih Men sections.

---

[1] Metaphorical expression meaning to swing. When the swing is high in the air one can for the moment imagine oneself an Immortal, only presently to swing back to earth again and find oneself once more an ordinary human being.

[2] 渭 陽, a place south-west of the present Feng-huang district in Hupeh.

CHAPTER III—THE THIRD MONTH

THIRD DAY OF THIRD MONTH

IT is commonly said that people who plant gourds must sow their seeds on the third day of the third month. Otherwise there will not be many that will mature.

HALL OF SPIRAL PEACHES (*P'an T'ao Kung* 蟠桃宫)

The Hall of Great Peace (T'ai P'ing Kung) is on the south side of the road to Tung Pien Men, where its gate overlooks the city moat. It is called the Hall of Spiral Peaches because there is an image inside of the Western Queen Mother (Hsi Wang Mu 西王母). Each year, beginning from the first day of the third month, the temple is opened for three days, when there are many sightseers. But in comparison with such places as Po Yün Kuan it is not as active.

> *Note :* Hsi Wang Mu is an important member of the Taoist pantheon, and is supposed to be the progenitor of the *yin* or female life force. Hence the peach, which is the Taoist symbol of immortality, forms part of the feast which she supposedly holds on the occasion of her birthday, at the time of the festival here mentioned. The name of the temple is derived from this fact. For further information about Hsi Wang Mu see H. A. Giles : *Who was Si Wang Mu?* in *Adversaria Sinica*, Shanghai, 1914. †

TEMPLE OF THE EASTERN PEAK (*Tung Yüeh Miao* 東嶽廟)

> *Note :* The Eastern Peak is China's famous sacred mountain, T'ai Shan, in Shantung, which, being situated in the eastern part of China, the quarter from which the sun, giver of life, rises, is supposed to be both the source of life, and hence the place where souls go after death. Throughout China there are many Taoist temples dedicated to " The Equal of Heaven " (T'ien Ch'i 天齊), who is the god of T'ai Shan, and who presides over the souls of the dead.

The Tung Yüeh Miao is about two *li* outside Ch'ao Yang Men. Every year, in addition to the first and fifteenth of every month, the temple is thrown open for half a month, beginning from the fifteenth day of the third month, when men and women assemble like clouds. The twenty-eighth day is especially busy, and in common parlance is called the time of Meeting to Brush-off Dust (*T'an Ch'en Hui* 撣塵會) (i.e., from the images). But actually it is the birthday of the great Emperor of the Eastern Peak.

> *Note :* This temple is also much frequented during the two weeks after New Year.
>
> †See page xviii of the Introduction to the Second Edition.

The temple has seventy-two shrines, each of which is presided over by its own deity. It is traditionally said that the deity at whose shrine the most prompt return is given (for one's acts),[1] is that of Yo Wu-mu,[2] who has extraordinary supernatural power. If all those who have received injuries and bear grudges leaving stained traces in their hearts, will come to this spot and make a solemn confession, they will have an especially speedy reward. In front of the steps (before Yo Fei) is the kneeling image of Ch'in Kuei,[3] and there is no one who sees it who does not spit upon it, so that now one can no longer distinguish his features.

In the rear hall is the Imperial Ruler Tzŭ T'ung,[4] who also has remarkable supernatural power, so that in years of the government examinations those going to pray to him follow each other in queues. At the right of the deity's throne is the image of a mule wnich is especially capable of curing people's illnesses : those who have a disease of the ear touch its ear ; those who have eye disease rub its eyes ; and those who have diseased feet stroke its feet.

East of this hall are several images in armor and helmets, whose bodies are half buried in the ground, and which tradition commonly says represent military generals of the Yang family.[5] But after all it is not really known what deities they are. Inside the temple is a Taoist stone tablet inscribed by Chao Meng-fu, Senior of the Hanlin Academy under the Yüan dynasty.[6] But although the characters themselves are genuine (products of that time), they are lacking in spirit, and I believe must have been cut out by some ordinary artisan.

According to the *Jih-hsia*, Tung Yüeh Miao was founded during the Yen Yo period (1314-1320) of the Yüan dynasty, in order to

---

[1] Here Taoism has adopted the Buddhist conception of Karma, i.e., that one's future destiny is rigidly determined by one's own good and bad deeds performed in this and previous incarnations.

[2] 岳武穆, i.e., the famous general Yo Fei (1103-1141), whom the Chinese have revered as a model of patriotism. He struggled valiantly for the Sung dynasty against the Chin Tartars, until intrigue at home brought about his imprisonment on a false charge of treason, and ultimate execution.

[3] 秦檜, the man whose intrigues led to Yo Fei's execution, and whom the Chinese on that account have ever execrated.

[4] 梓潼, i.e., Wen Ch'ang 文昌, the God of Literature.

[5] Headed by the noted general Yang Yeh 楊業, who fought valiantly against the Liao Tartars under Emperor T'ai Tsung (976-997) of the Sung dynasty.

[6] A noted calligrapher and painter, especially of horses, who lived 1254-1322.

worship T'ien Ch'i, the Loving and Sage Emperor of the Eastern
Peak. In the Ming dynasty, during the Cheng T'ung period (1436-
1449), the buildings were enlarged and the two side wings with their
seventy-two shrines were built. Later on a traveling lodge was made
for the Imperial concubines (for times when they might pass here).
During the present dynasty, in the thirty-seventh year of K'ang Hsi
(1698), the people living here were not careful and the temple was
burned down. A special expenditure from the Imperial private funds
was made to repair it, and in three years the damage was made good,
while the former appearance of the halls and side galleries was made
more elaborate. In the twenty-sixth year of Ch'ien Lung (1761) there
were further repairs, and the lay-out was made still more imposing,
so that even unto the present day, when Imperial visits are made to
the Eastern Tombs (where several of the Manchu Emperors are buried),
the Emperor must here offer incense and take food.[1]

MONASTERY OF CLEAR POOLS AND WILD MULBERRY
(T'an Che Ssŭ 潭柘寺)

T'an Che Ssŭ is in the region of the Turbid River (Hun Ho),
west of Stone Prospect Mountain (Shih Ching Shan), and north of
Pear Orchard Village (Li Yüan Chuang), more than eighty *li* distant
from Peking. Each year, beginning from the first day of the third
month, the temple is opened for half a month, when incense fires
are very numerous. The temple lies in the midst of many mountains
and is surrounded by nine peaks, while inside of it there tortuously
meanders a flowing spring which disappears outside the gate. There
is a gingko[2] tree which is commonly named the Tree of Emperors and
Kings (*Ti Wang Shu* 帝王樹), and which is more than one hundred
feet high and several tens of human arm-spans in circumference.
Truly is it a thing of centuries and millenniums !

> *Note*: There is a curious story about this tree which explains its unusual designation, and
> which our author omits, probably because he was himself a Manchu and so feared lest
> he might offend the ruling house. According to this story, this tree would herald
> the accession of a new Emperor by putting forth a new sprout from its trunk, while
> the Emperor's death would likewise be forewarned by the dying of the sprout.

[1] It was here also that Imperial concubines, who ordinarily rarely left the Palace, would receive
visits from their families in the traveling lodge described above.

[2] Japanese name derived from the Chinese *yin kuo* 銀菓 meaning silver fruit. These trees are
extremely long-lived, and are often planted around tombs.

猗玗流觴

MONASTERY OF CLEAR POOLS AND WILD MULBERRY (T'AN CHE SSŬ)

Cut out of the stone floor of the central pavilion is seen a channel for running water. This channel
has the form of the face of a *chi han* 猗玗, a variety of savage wild dog. In front lies the famous
Bamboo Court. The making of curving water-courses of this sort originated from the pastime
of floating cups of wine down a winding stream to picnic guests waiting below, as shown
in the picture.

Furthermore there are magnolias, luxuriant bamboos, pines,
cedars, and bodhi trees,[1] all of which are likewise several centuries old.
An unexcelled spot, in truth!

Formerly the discipline and rules (of this Buddhist temple) were
extremely severe, and no meat or wine could enter, but in recent times
wines and roast meats are to be found in confused abundance, (brought

---

[1] So named because it was supposedly under this tree that Sakyamuni Buddha received his
enlightenment.

by visitors), and there has been no return to the purity of earlier
times.   There are two supernatural snakes here called the Big Green
and Little Green. . . . . As to the wild mulberry tree, only a few feet
of it are still preserved,[1] and this, together with the stone tablet of
the Yüan dynasty Princess and nun, Miao Yen,[2] praying to the Buddha,
are both old relics.   All who come to the temple should look at these
several things.

According to the *Jih-hsia*, T'an Che Ssŭ was. . . . . called Admirable
Happiness (Chia Fu 嘉 福) during the Chin dynasty (A.D. 265-316),
and Dragon Spring (Lung Ch'üan 龍 泉) during the T'ang (618-906).
A Peking proverb says : " First there was T'an Che Ssŭ, and afterward
there was Peking." [3] All of which shows how very old the temple is.

During the K'ang Hsi period (1662-1722) of the present dynasty
it was renamed Temple of Peaks and Clouds (Hsiu Yün Ssŭ 岫 雲 寺).
The temple formerly had a spring at the foundations of the (present
main) Buddhist hall, which formed the " pool " (*t'an*, which with the
che tree described above, gives T'an Che Ssŭ its name).   Once when
during the T'ang dynasty, a Master of the Hua Yen Sect was preaching
the Buddhist law on the mountain, a divine dragon came out of this
pool to make the temple, and after a single evening of great wind and
rain, the pool was changed into level ground.   Now the pool has disappeared, but water continues to pour forth without ceasing.   The
wild mulberry (*che*) tree has long since decayed, but its remaining
height of seven or eight feet is covered over with a tiled pavilion.   The
dragon has gone away, but its offspring still remain, green in color, five
feet in length, and as thick as a cup.   At times they show themselves.

Note : These are the two snakes referred to above.

ORDINATION TERRACE TEMPLE (*Chieh T'ai Ssŭ* 戒 臺 寺)

All who go to T'an Che Ssŭ should likewise go to Chieh T'ai
Ssŭ.   Chieh T'ai does not have any definite pilgrim season, but on

---

[1] The petrified trunk of this *che* 柘 tree, which has helped to give T'an Che Ssŭ its name,
still stands in a courtyard protected by an enclosure.

[2] 妙 嚴, the daughter of Kublai Khan (1280-1294), who died in this temple, and was noted for
her piety.

[3] *Hsien yu T'an Che, hou yu Pei Ching* 先 有 潭 柘, 後 有 北 京.

松玩臺戒

ORDINATION TERRACE TEMPLE (CHIEH T'AI SSŬ)

Through the front balcony projects the famous curving pine. Notice that the stone tablet
which now supports the pine, inscribed with the characters 卧龍松 *Wo Lung Sung* (Sleeping
Dragon Pine), had not yet been erected when this drawing was made.

the sixth day of the sixth month there is a meeting for airing the holy
sutras in the sun. Though some people go to witness this, they are
very few, probably because at this time the weather is hot, besides
which there is a great deal of rain.

The temple is also called the Temple of Ten Thousand Ages
(Wan Shou Ssŭ), and is south-east of T'an Che Ssŭ. It is outstanding
for its white pines, and so when Pekinese speak about pilgrimages,
they must always mention it in one breath with T'an Che Ssŭ.

According to the *Jih-hsia*, Wan Shou Ssŭ lies on Horse Saddle Mountain (Ma An Shan). It was founded in the T'ang dynasty during the Wu Te period (618-626), and was then called Wise Assembly Temple (Hui Chü Ssŭ 慧 聚 寺). In the Ming dynasty during the Cheng T'ung period (1436-1449), this was changed to its present name. It has some couplets written by K'ang Hsi and Ch'ien Lung, and a platform of ordination for new priests, which was first inaugurated by the monk Fa Chün during the Hsien Yung period (1066-1073) of the Liao dynasty. In the Ming time during the Cheng T'ung period, Ju Huan, a Master of the Legalist Sect,[1] was commanded by Imperial decree to expound the Buddhist discipline, and to erect a platform for this purpose. This platform is inside the big hall, and is made of white stone. Behind the temple are the Five Caves of Great Antiquity, Kuanyin (who is the beloved Buddhist goddess of mercy), Hua Yang,[2] P'ang Chüan, and Sun Pin.[3] Four or five *li* west of the temple is the Peak of Extreme Joyfulness (Chi Lo Feng).

MONASTERY OF EXALTED HEAVEN (*T'ien T'ai Ssŭ* 天 台 寺)

T'ien T'ai Mountain is at Mo Shih K'ou, west of the Capital, and may be reached by carriages and horses. It is a mountain lying behind Ts'ui Wei Shan.[4] Every year on the eighteenth day of the third month the temple of the same name is opened, on which day incense fires are very numerous. The gate of the temple lies at the foot of the southern mountain, while the temple itself lies on the height of the northern mountain, the two being separated by about a *li*. By the side of the mountain are three or four gushing springs

---

[1] 律 宗, a sect founded during the T'ang dynasty, which shows special proclivities for Buddhist biographies and history, and church government.

[2] 化 陽 is here a mistake for 華 陽. This is the name of a district in Shensi which was once governed by Hsin Jung 辛 戌, younger brother of the Empress Hsüan, who was wife of Hui Wen Wang (reigned 337-311 B.C.) of the State of Ch'in. Later he came to this cave, which he named after his former district, and where he lived as a recluse.

[3] 龐 涓 and 孫 臏. These two men studied military science together during the fourth century B.C., but later became deadly rivals, the former serving the State of Wei 魏 and the latter the State of Ch'i. P'ang caused Sun to undergo the punishment of having both legs amputated, but later was defeated by the latter in battle and committed suicide.

[4] 翠 微 山, i.e., Pa Ta Ch'u in the Western Hills, from which it may be pleasantly reached on foot.

which flow without stopping. As to the so called Demon King (Mo Wang 魔 王), what is said about it is all wild baseless talk.

Note: Our author here indignantly refuses to enter into a discussion concerning the famous " mummy " to be found in this temple, a remarkably fine and realistic image of an elderly man, clad in Imperial yellow robes. This image is supposedly the mummified body of Emperor Shun Chih (1644-1661), who, according to the legend, secretly abdicated and retired to this temple to become a monk, after the death of a Chinese girl with whom he had been much in love. This story has been thoroughly disproved by Sir R. F. Johnston, however, who in his turn identifies the image with a mad monk who gained a great deal of fame for the temple until his death there in 1710, and on whom Ch'ien Lung later conferred the above-mentioned title, " Demon King." *Cf.* his *The Romance of an Emperor*, in *The New China Review*, Vol. II, No. 2, pp. 180-194.

SEASON FOR CHANGING HATS AND HAIRPINS

Every year in the third month comes the season for changing to cool hats, while in the eighth month comes the changing back to warm hats. The arrival of the time is decided by the Ministry of Rites, which presents a request to the Emperor (for his ratification). Usually it falls somewhere around the twentieth day. At the time of changing to cooler hats, women all likewise change to jade hairpins, while at the time of changing to warmer hats, they all change to gold hairpins.

YELLOW TROUT AND 'BIG-HEAD' FISH

Every year during the third month Peking has yellow trout, otherwise known as " stone-head fish " (*shih shou yü* 石 首 魚). At the time when they first reach the capital, the Supervisor of Ch'ung Wen Men (i.e., Hatamen gate)[1] sends some of these fish according to rule to the Emperor. If this were not done, they would be illicit merchandise, and even though there might be persons who brought them secretly bound under their belts, they would not dare to sell them. In the fourth month come the " big-head " fish (*ta t'ou yü* 大 頭 魚 or *Gadus macrocephalus*, a kind of cod), also known as *hai chi* 海 鰤, the flavor of which is somewhat inferior to that of the yellow trout, and which are not presented to the Emperor.

---

[1] This was the Hatamen Octroi, which collected taxes for the whole city.

CHAPTER IV—THE FOURTH MONTH

DISTRIBUTION OF BEANS TO ACCUMULATE GOOD KARMA
(*She Yüan Tou* 捨 緣 豆)

ON the eighth day of the fourth month such people of the Capital as love virtue take several pints of green and yellow beans, and pick the beans up one by one, putting them down again a little distance away, reciting each time the name of (Amitābha) Buddha. When this ceremony is over, they boil the beans and distribute them (to anyone who happens to be passing by). The city people call this " giving away karma-accumulating beans," because it is done to store up good karma for future incarnations.[1]

According to the *Jih-hsia*, Peking Buddhist priests, and other people who would invoke Buddha's name, kept a record of the number of invocations by counting beans, (as they were passed from one bowl to another) immediately (after each invocation). On the eighth day of the fourth month, which is the Buddha's birthday, they would cook beans with only a little salt, and would stop people on the street, inviting them to partake.

This was done so as to accumulate karma, and to-day we still follow this old custom.

TEMPLE OF TEN THOUSAND AGES (*Wan Shou Ssŭ* 萬 壽 寺)

Wan Shou Ssŭ is five or six *li* outside Hsi Chih Men, where its gate overlooks the Long Canal (*Ch'ang Ho* 長 河, which flows from the Summer Palace to the city). It is the place where the Empress Dowager offers sacrifice so as to secure felicity. Each year, beginning from the first day of the fourth month, the temple is opened for half a month, when there are a great many pilgrims. Women and men in colorful costumes come in lines along the paths, where the wind sounds through the willows and makes undulations in the wheat, washing

---

[1] The word *yüan* 緣 in the Chinese phrase is really the Chinese rendering of the Sanskrit word *pratyaya*, meaning causation, whereas the Sanskrit term, *karma*, is usually expressed in Chinese by the word *yeh* 業. Here, however, the meaning of the phrase is that the distribution of beans will act as a causative force which will create good karma, and so will serve to improve the lot of the giver in his next incarnation. Hence it is translated in this way.

the bosom clear of one's bad feelings. Especially on a genial day with clear weather, when there is a kind and beneficent wind, this is truly an unexcelled spot in the western suburbs.

According to the *Jih-hsia*, Wan Shou Ssŭ is west of the Kuang Yüan sluice, and was founded during the Ming dynasty in the fifth year of Wan Li (1577). It was repaired twice during the present dynasty, in the sixteenth and twenty-sixth years of Ch'ien Lung (1751 and 1761). Inside the main gate are bell and drum towers, and a hall of the Heavenly Kings or Lokapalās.[1] Behind this hall is the Hall of Ten Thousand Ages (Wan Shou Ko), in the back of which is a Meditation Hall. To the rear of this rises an imitation hill, above which is a hall of Kuanyin, while below is a cave of Ti Ts'ang (the Bodhisattva of the Underworld). Behind the hill stands a hall of Amitābha Buddha, and a hall of the Three Sages.[2] Still farther back is a rear two-storey building, in front of which once grew pines and cypresses all several centuries old, but which were destroyed by fire in the first year of Kuang Hsü (1875). Farthest back of all is a vegetable garden with two pumps. In the twentieth year of Kuang Hsü (1895) the Imperial rest-room was repaired and made into one enclosure together with the vegetable garden.

Note : Since 1934 this temple has been used to house one of the several divisions of North-eastern University, which was removed from Mukden after the Japanese occupation of Manchuria. Several of its halls have been stripped of their images and converted into class-rooms, while most of the priests have gone elsewhere. As a result the place has lost many of the features which made it such a notable example of Buddhist temples.

WESTERN PEAK (*Hsi Ting* 西 項)

The Temple of the Goddess of the Western Peak (Hsi Ting Niang Niang Miao 西 項 娘 娘 廟) is eight or nine *li* west of Wan Shou Ssŭ, and each year, beginning from the first day of the fourth month, the temple is opened for half a month, when it is equal in activity to the latter. The images of the Four Heavenly Kings at the main gate

---

[1] T'ien Wang 天王. These are the four fierce-looking guardians who stand inside the entrance of Buddhist temples, and who also preside over the four quarters of the universe and the four seas.

[2] Sakyamuni as representing the Buddha or Fo 佛, Vairocana as representing the Buddhist doctrine or *fa* 法, and Loshana as representing the Buddhist society of monks or *seng* 僧.

seem alive in their spirit and manner, looking so fierce as to be terrifying. Beneath their thrones are eight monstrous devils (who support them) and who can also so startle people, that everyone leading small children here covers their eyes when passing through. The temple has seventy-two shrines, the deities of which are painted rather than sculptured. Every time the temple is thrown open, the Emperor specially delegates a great official to offer incense, in the same way as at Ya Chi Shan,[1] whereas other places do not have this honor.

> *Note :* This temple has now fallen into ruins, but the murals mentioned by the author still exist and are well worth seeing. The temple is situated in the village of Lan Tien Ch'ang 藍靛廠 on the Long Canal.

According to the *Jih-hsia*, the temple. . . . . was founded during the Wan Li period (1573-1619) of the Ming dynasty, and repaired during the present dynasty in the fifty-first year of K'ang Hsi (1712), when its name was changed to that of the Hall of Vast Virtue (Kuang Jen Kung 廣仁宮).

MOUNTAIN OF THE MYSTERIOUS PEAK (*Miao Feng Shan* 妙峯山)

The Temple of the Princess of the Colored Clouds (Pi Hsia Yüan Chün Miao) at Miao Feng Shan is more than eighty *li* north-west of Peking.[2] Besides this the mountain path is over forty *li*, making a total of over one hundred and thirty *li*. It lies in the district of Ch'ang P'ing.

Each year, beginning from the first day of the fourth month, the temple is thrown open for half a month, when incense fires are extremely numerous. Whenever there is rain before the opening, it is called " rain to purify the mountain." The temple lies in the midst of many mountains, and is on one lonely lofty peak, to which the path twists as it ascends, snail-like, so that those who are in front can look down on the heads of those who are behind, and those behind can see the feet of those in front. From the beginning of the pilgrimage season to the end, continuously night and day, there is

---

[1] On this temple, *cf.* p. 40.

[2] Pi Hsia Yüan Chün 碧霞元君 is the daughter of the god of T'ai Shan (T'ien Ch'i), and was created by the Taoists of the Sung dynasty to counteract the growing influence of the great Buddhist goddess, Kuanyin. She is the chief of a number of Taoist goddesses who send children to the childless, cure eye diseases, are the patrons of wet-nurses, and in other ways are associated with women.

no halt in the stream of people and no cessation of the smoke of incense. Truly a remarkable sight!

The main gate of the temple is on the south side. There are a main and a rear hall, while in front of the rear hall rises a rocky eminence, which appears to be Miao Feng Shan's stone summit. There are also three or four cypresses which seem to be several centuries old. East of the temple are halls of the God of Joy (Hsi Shen), of Kuanyin, and of Fu Mo (伏 魔, another name for Kuan Ti, the God of War). North of the temple is a Pavilion for the Incense of the Returners. The temple has no stone tablets, and there is no means of delving into its origin, but nevertheless it has been existing at least from the time of Yung Cheng (1723-1735) and Ch'ien Lung (1736-1795) onward. What a pity there are no records concerning it!

Note: It is remarkable that so few records exist telling about this, easily the most popular of all pilgrimages around Peking. Jung Keng 容 庚, in an article devoted to the origin of the Miao Feng Shan pilgrimage, quotes the account given here by our author in full, as being almost the only detailed description of the place. He gives however, another reference to Miao Feng Shan which shows that it was a center for pilgrims at least as early as 1629, so that its origin goes back to the Ming dynasty. Cf. Miao Feng Shan, pp. 124 f., a book in Chinese giving a detailed study of the subject, published under the general editorship of Ku Chieh-kang 顧 頡 剛 in 1928. Ku Chieh-kang in this same book, pp. 26 f., shows, however, that it was only in the Ch'ing dynasty that Miao Feng Shan could have become really popular. During the Ming dynasty the temples of the Princess of the Colored Clouds which were most visited were five situated closer to Peking, popularly known as the Northern, Southern, Eastern, Western, and Central Peaks, all of which are described in the present work.

The pilgrim routes have increased as time has gone on, and consist of the southern route via San Chia Tien; the central route via the Temple of Great Enlightenment (Ta Chüeh Ssŭ); and the northern route via Pei An Ho. That of the Hall of the Stone Buddha (Shih Fo Tien) is called the old northern route, but in recent times none is so crowded as that of Pei An Ho. Here the jets of smoke from human dwellings are innumerable; carts and horses jam the streets; and the multitude of lights and fires during the night gleam like stars. If we were to count the people who come yearly over all the different roads, there would probably be a total of several hundreds of thousands, and if we estimated the money expended, it also would probably be several hundreds of thousands of taels.

The number of incense fires here truly may be put as first in the entire world.[1]

FORKED HAIR-TUFT MOUNTAIN (*Ya Chi Shan* 了 髻 山)

The Temple of the Princess of the Colored Clouds at Ya Chi Shan is (eighty odd *li*) north-east of Peking, in the Huai Jou district. Each year, beginning from the first day of the fourth month, the temple is opened for half a month, but its activity is second to that of Miao Feng Shan, though its mountainous scenery surpasses it. People of the Capital call it the Eastern Mountain.

NORTHERN AND EASTERN PEAKS (*Pei Ting* 北 頂 *and Tung Ting* 東 頂)

The Temple of the Princess of the Colored Clouds at the Northern Peak is outside Te Sheng Men about three *li* north-east of the Earth Wall, and each year during the fourth month it has a temple fair, at which all kinds of agricultural implements for everyday use are sold, those who go there being mostly farmers. The Eastern Peak is outside Tung Chih Men, and is similar to the Northern Peak.

ELM-SEED CAKES (*Yü Ch'ien Kao* 榆 錢 糕)

In the third month when the elms first have their seeds, these are collected and boiled with sugar and flour to make elm-seed cakes. While in the fourth month there are cakes made of roses, called rose cakes (*mei-kuei ping* 玫 瑰 餅), and of wistaria blossoms, called wistaria cakes (*t'eng-lo ping* 藤 蘿 餅). These are all things eaten according to their season.

ORIOLES

In the latter part of the fourth month, when the time for spring flowers is soon over, it is easy to have a feeling of sadness (at the thought of the departure of spring). Then in the shadows of the willows the orioles call softly, with a sound like that of the playing of reed-organs, music (such as one would listen to when sitting in a quiet place) with a measure of wine and some oranges. After some-

---

[1] This is one of the most picturesque of all pilgrimages around Peking, and what is especially lovely is to see the pilgrims returning, gay with the many colored paper flowers, bats, etc., which they have bought at the temple and stuck in their hair and hats to signify that they have made the pilgrimage.

what more than one month they go away, for they cannot remain long. An old poem says :

"When the orioles let out their cries, the mulberries become beautiful. When the orioles no longer sing, the mulberries have become ripe." [1]

These words are in exact accord with this period in Peking.

RUSH SHOOTS AND CHERRIES

During the fourth month shoots of the rush (*phragmites communis*) and cherries are both eaten, and are extremely sweet and fine. An old poem says :

"At the time when the rush shoots appear, the willow catkins fly about. When the red cherries become ripe, the wind is cool through the wheat." [2]

This too is in close accordance with the Peking calendar.

COLD FRIED PASTRY (*Liang Ch'ao Mien* 涼炒麵)

In the fourth month, when the wheat first becomes ripe, dough is fried, mixed with sugar, and eaten, this pastry being called *liang ch'ao mien*.

ROSES AND PEONIES

The rose has a rich mauve color, and its sweet fragrance well suits people's tastes. Householders all love it, and in the fourth month when its blossoms open, the shouts of its vendors on the streets come now softly, now loudly, so that when one hears them on rising in the morning, they have a great deal of character.

Peonies (of the small type, whose stems are not woody) are produced in Feng T'ai (a small place south-west and not far from Peking), and when in season appear massed together wherever one looks. In the fourth month when the blossoms are still buds, the cut stalks are sold. Everywhere throughout the city there are then such varieties as the "Concubine Yang," [3] and "doltish white (*sha pai* 傻白)."

These two flowers are exceedingly regular (in their growth), so that even though heat be applied to warm them, they cannot change their time and open before the proper season. Among flowers they are indeed the ones that resist the demands of man.

---

[1] *Huang li liu ming, sang chen mei* ; 黃鸝留鳴，桑椹美.

Huang li chi ming, tse sang chen ch'ui shu. 黃鸝即鳴，則桑椹垂熟.

[2] *Lu hsün sheng shih, liu hsü fei* ; 蘆筍生時，柳絮飛.

Tzŭ ying t'ao shu, mai feng liang. 紫櫻桃熟，麥風涼.

[3] Yang Kuei Fei, who died A.D. 756. She was a concubine of Emperor Ming Huang, and China's most famous beauty. Under her spell Ming Huang forgot the cares of state and gave himself up to amusement, with the result that a disastrous civil war broke out which, though finally suppressed, led to the decline of the T'ang dynasty.

CHAPTER V—THE FIFTH MONTH

Dragon-Boat or 'Upright Sun' Festival (*Tuan Yang* 端 陽)

PEKINESE call the festival of the fifth month the *Tuan Yang*, the fifth day (the day on which this festival falls) being the Single Fifth (*tan wu* 單 五) of the fifth month. Probably this word *tan* is a corruption of the sound of the word *tuan*. Every year, preceding and on the *Tuan Yang*, noble families give presents to one another of *tsung-tzŭ* 粽 子,[1] to which are added such things as cherries, mulberries, water-chestnuts, peaches, apricots, cakes of the Five Poisonous Creatures (*wu tu ping* 五 毒 餅), and rose-cakes.[2] But for offerings to be made to the gods or to the ancestors, simply the *tsung-tzŭ*, together with cherries and mulberries, are the proper things to give, the idea being to offer foods of the season.

THE FIVE POISONOUS CREATURES

According to the *Hsü-ch'i-hsieh-chi*, Ch'ü Yüan on the fifth day of the fifth month cast himself into the Mi Lo River.[3] The people of Ch'u[4] mourned for him, and every year on this day would put rice into bamboo tubes, which they released on the waters as offerings to

---

[1] Triangular masses of rice or glutinous millet, wrapped in leaves, which are especially made for this festival.

[2] These five poisonous creatures are the centipede (shown winged and footless here!), scorpion, snake, lizard, and toad, effigies of which are molded on top of these cakes, probably with the idea that the bite of these creatures will thus be avoided. This is a time when the heat of summer, with its accompanying vapors and pestilences, has arrived. Hence everything possible is done on the *Tuan Yang* festival to ward off disease and evil influences.

[3] Ch'ü Yüan, author of the *Li Sao*, is one of China's most famous poets. Becoming disgusted with the political events of his time, he abandoned the human world after having made several vain protests, and finally committed suicide *circa* 288 B.C. The Mi Lo River. into which he is said to have thrown himself, flows into Tung T'ing Lake in Hunan.

[4] Ch'ü Yüan's native State, occupying much of present Hunan, Hupeh, Anhuei, Chekiang, and Kiangsi.

渡競門津

DRAGON BOATS

him. The tops of these tubes would be closed with lily leaves, tied up with colored silk, so that the scaly dragon would not steal them. And this is the origin of the *tsung-tzǔ*.

Note: This is probably a myth. The *Tuan Yang* festival comes at a time when rain is needed for the growing crops, and the *tsung-tzǔ* originally were probably offerings to the scaly dragon, who is the controller of rain, to induce him to bring rainfall. Likewise races take place in the south, though not so much in the north, between long "dragon boats," which have carved dragon heads and are paddled by many men. This custom supposedly began with the attempt to discover Ch'ü Yüan's drowned body, but it too probably originated much earlier in an attempt, through sympathetic magic, to induce by means of the dragon boat contests, the dragons of the air to struggle together and so send down rain.

REALGAR WINE (*Hsiung Huang Chiu* 雄黃酒)

At every arrival of the *Tuan Yang*, beginning with the first day, people take (a small amount of) realgar, mix it with wine, dry it in the sun, and paint it on the foreheads, noses, and ears of small children, to ward off poisonous creatures.

Note: One often sees at this time the character *wang* 王 (meaning " king ") painted on children's foreheads. This character supposedly appears among the markings on the forehead of the tiger, which is the protector, *par excellence*, against evil creatures.

CHARMS OF THE HEAVENLY MASTER (*T'ien Shih Fu* 天 師 符) [1]

Every year at the time of the *Tuan Yang*, shops have yellow streamers a foot long, covered with vermilion seal impressions, [2] or perhaps painted with figures of the " Heavenly Master " or of Chung K'uei, [3] or with the forms of the five poisonous creatures, which serve as charms. These are hung up and sold, and the people of the Capital compete with one another in buying them. They are pasted on the second gate of one's house to ward off evil influences.

According to the *Li I Chih* (Chapter fifteen) of the *Hou Han Shu*, a red string and seal impressions of five colors were at that period displayed on gates and doors on the fifth day of the fifth month to stop evil vapors. Is this not the origin of the " Heavenly Master " charms ?

CALAMUS AND MUGWORT PLANTS

On the *Tuan Yang* day (leaves of) calamus (*ch'ang p'u* 菖 蒲) and mugwort (*ai tzŭ* 艾 子) are put up at the sides of gates to avert what is unpropitious. This, too, is a survival from the ancient belief that the mugwort leaves look like a tiger, and the calamus leaves like a sword.

COLORED SILK TIGERS STRUNG TOGETHER

Every year at the *Tuan Yang* festival the clever ones in the women's quarters cut out of silk gauze such things as small tigers, *tsung-tzŭ*

---

[1] The " Taoist Pope " of the Chang family. *Cf.* Note on p. 16.

[2] The color red, not only in China but in other countries, has the power to protect against evil.

[3] Once the T'ang Emperor, Ming Huang (712-756), while suffering from a fever, is said to have had a dream in which he was tormented by an imp. But suddenly a tall figure appeared which tore out the imp's eye and ate it. On being asked by the Emperor who he was, the figure replied that he was a physician who during a former reign had been unjustly defrauded of his rights in the government examinations. After this he had committed suicide, whereupon the Emperor of that time had ordered him to be buried with special honors. Out of gratitude he had then sworn ever to protect future rulers. On awaking, Ming Huang found his fever gone. He had the picture of his protector, Chung K'uei, painted, and canonized him with the title : " Great Spiritual Chaser of Demons for the Whole Empire."

CHUNG K'UEI, THE DEMON CHASER

(the triangular rice puddings described above), gourds, cherries, and mulberries, and string them together on a colored silk thread. These they suspend from the heads of their hairpins, or tie on the backs of small children. An old poem speaking of " A jade swallow on the head of a hairpin ; a trifling mugwort tiger," [1] refers to this.

According to what the *Feng-su-t'ung* says, on the fifth day of the fifth month colored silks would be tied on the back to ward off demons and soldiers, and would likewise prevent people from catching infectious diseases. One name for them was " threads of long life," while another name was " threads for prolonging life."

CHILD WITH
SILK CHARMS
OR 'TIGERS'

COLORED SILK GOURDS

Also on the *Tuan Yang* day figures of all kinds of gourds are cut out of colored silks and paper. These are pasted in an inverted position above gates and gate-screens so as to pour out thereby all poisonous vapors. But after the fifth day of the fifth month they are taken off and thrown away.

Note: The gourd, being used by Chinese apothecaries as a receptacle for drugs, suggests the power of healing, and hence is much used at this season as a protection against noxious influences. Notice the gourd from which medicinal vapors rise, in the painting of Li T'ieh Kuai facing p. 105.

IMPERIAL DISTRIBUTION OF GRASS-LINEN

The princes, dukes, and great officials of the Court, at the *Tuan Yang* time all receive through the kindness of the Emperor presents of grass-linen and of round painted fans.

INSPECTION TOUR OF THE ' GOD OF THE CITY '. (*Ch'eng Huang* 城 隍)

Note: Every town has one of these Ch'eng Huang, or " God of Ramparts and Moats, " who has jurisdiction over its spiritual affairs, just as the human magistrate controls worldly matters. Often they are local heroes who have become deified, and each year, as here described, they are taken out to inspect their domain.

On the twenty-second day of the fourth month the City God of the district of Wan P'ing (in which lies the western part of Peking) goes out on a tour of inspection, while on the first day of the fifth month the City God of the district of Ta Hsing (in which lies the eastern

---

[1] *Yü yen ch'ai t'ou, ai hu ch'ing.* 玉 燕 釵 頭 艾 虎 輕.

portion of Peking) does likewise. At the time of these tours they
are each of them borne in a chair on the shoulders of eight men, who
lift the images up on rattan poles and so move along. (On such
occasions are always to be seen) persons who " sacrifice their bodies "
(*she shen* 捨 身) by acting as "horse-slaves"; or as fanners (of the City
God); or who lead the way with their arms pierced by iron hooks
from which lanterns are suspended; or who carry a wooden cangue
and bear chains, wearing a fierce appearance as if they were criminals.
Besides these, there are men at the side of the spirit's chair dressed up
as judges and as demon soldiers. Slowly they move step by step,
and fail not indeed to give an impression of a divine progress which
instils good behavior.

> Note : Persons who " sacrifice their bodies " are those who perform penance in fulfilment
> of some vow made when the god was called upon for help of some sort. Thus the
> " horse slave " crawls on the ground on all fours with an imitation saddle on his back
> and a bit in his teeth. Many of these forms of penance (including that of persons who
> kotow every third step) may still be seen to-day on the way to Miao Feng Shan during
> the pilgrim season, though the tours of the City God, in Peking at least, are now no
> longer held.

ITINERANT PLAYER SOCIETIES (*Kuo Hui* 過 會)

These itinerant societies are comprised of unoccupied people of
Peking who dress themselves up as. . . . . [here follows a list of technical
terms of the different types of performers to be seen on pilgrimages
and at temple fairs, such as male dancers dressed as women, stilt
walkers, and lion-dancers, i.e., men who put on imitation lion costumes
and prance, jump, and perform acrobatic feats like lions]. If these
societies meet one of the tours of inspection of the City God, or any
other kind of temple meeting, they straightway begin to perform
and sing. Then the onlookers mass themselves like a wall, and it
is very easy to start some kind of trouble. Hence whenever such
societies encounter a conscientious Commandant of the Gendarmerie,
he puts a stop to them as soon as he sees them.

TEMPLE OF THE CITY GOD OF THE CAPITAL
(*Tu Ch'eng Huang Miao* 都 城 隍 廟)

The Tu Ch'eng Huang Miao is inside Hsüan Wu Men, west of
Kou Yen, on the north side of Ch'eng Huang Miao Chieh. Each year,

臨清社火

ITINERANT PLAYER SOCIETIES AT A TEMPLE FESTIVAL

beginning from the first day of the fifth month, there is a temple fair
for ten days, at which all kinds of children's toys are sold. It has
nothing especially remarkable, and visitors are few.[1]

According to the *Jih-hsia*, the Tu Ch'eng Huang Miao used to
have a temple fair during the Ming dynasty, on the first, fifteenth, and
twenty-third days. The displays on these fair days were very numerous,
with everything used in daily human life, both delicate and coarse,
fully prepared. Visitors who came to this fair carrying money would

---

[1] This fair is now no longer held.

in a short time be richly supplied with purchases. Fine books, paintings, and curios both genuine and false, were haphazardly displayed, besides which were carved lacquer and second-hand objects which had come out of the Palace and had afterward been renovated. Originally the prices of these would be very little, but after their renovation they would go up ten times.

As to porcelain, the most valuable was that of the Ch'eng Hua period (1465-1487), next to which were the tea and winecups of the Hsüan Te period (1426-1435). Originally these did not exceed a few taels in price, but later when they became (known as) winecups of the (Imperial) kilns, they would reach a value of several hundred taels. The Hsüan Te incense burners, such as were presented as offerings (to the gods), were also generally of this order.

The temple goes back to Shih Tsu (Kublai Khan) of the Yüan dynasty, having been founded in the seventeenth year of the Chih Yüan period (1280). It was repaired during the Ming dynasty, and again during the present dynasty in the fourth year of Yung Cheng (1726), and in the twenty-eighth year of Ch'ien Lung (1763). In the first year of Kuang Hsü (1875) the temple was burned down, its stone tablets all destroyed, and the images of the City Gods of the Capitals of each of the provinces (which had also stood in this temple) were completely obliterated. At present only the main hall has been restored so as to permit the carrying out of the spring and autumn sacrifices, while the remaining parts are still completely dilapidated, as of that time.

SOUTHERN PEAK (Nan Ting 南 頂)

The Temple of the Princess of the Colored Clouds at the Southern Peak is five or six li outside Yung Ting Men. On the left and right, facing the west, are two p'ailou, the left one of which bears the words : " Prolific and long-lived " (Kuang sheng ch'ang yang 廣 生 長 養), while the right one bears the words : " Well-nourished and expanding " (Ch'ün yü tzŭ fan 羣 育 滋 蕃). These (phrases of good omen) were both written by the Emperor himself when the place was repaired in the thirty-eighth year of Ch'ien Lung (1773).

Every year, beginning from the first day of the fifth month, the temple is opened for ten days, when men and women come in swarms.[1] Though the temple itself is mean and in poor condition, there are pavilions (on the island) in the middle of the stream and on the small earth hill, with mat coverings, where one may sit and take refreshment. Toward evening when the people disperse, many of them go to Ta Sha Tzŭ K'ou (about half a *li* east and outside of Yung Ting Men) to look at the horse races.

According to the *Ch'en-yüan Shih-lüeh*, the stream to the south of the Southern Peak is called Cold Water River (Liang Shui Ho), and the name of the bridge there is Everlastingly Settled Bridge (Yung Ting Ch'iao). The earth hill is called Nine Dragon Hill (Chiu Lung Shan) and was formed when Cold Water River was dredged during the reign of Ch'ien Lung. It was planted around with many peach and willow trees, and pilgrims who came when the temple was open would all sit down with their winecups and drink in groups below the trees. But in recent times although the hill still remains, the peach and willow trees have all been destroyed.

TEN LI RIVER (*Shih Li Ho* 十 里 河)

The temple of Kuan Ti (the God of War) at Shih Li Ho lies outside Kuang Chu Men. Every year, beginning from the eleventh day of the fifth month, the temple is opened for three days, during which time actors come each year to perform according to invariable custom.[2]

JASPER TERRACE (*Yao T'ai* 瑤 台)[3]

The Yao T'ai is outside Cheng Yang Men (better known as Ch'ien Men gate) at the Black Kiln Factory (Hei Yao Ch'ang, name of a street leading toward the marshy open land in the extreme south city not far west of the Altar of Agriculture). Every year at the coming of the fifth month cool mat coverings are put up where tea is served, as places where people who come may climb up and look around at the view. This too is a remainder from the past in the south city.

---

[1] This fair has now been abandoned.

[2] This date has since been changed to the thirteenth and twenty-fourth days of the sixth month.

[3] A literary name given to places supposedly inhabited by immortals.

According to the *Jih-hsia*, Hei Yao Ch'ang is the place where tiles were made during the Ming dynasty. The present dynasty also ordered its kiln workers to work this kiln, but later on it fell into disuse. The ground here undulates in small hills high and low, and reeds and small islets of varying sort (appear amid the interspersed waters). People of the Capital are ever assembling here to climb up and see the view.

SWORD-GRINDING RAIN (*Mo Tao Yü* 磨 刀 雨)

A Peking proverb says : " The period of great dryness does not extend beyond the thirteenth of the fifth month." [1] This probably has reference to the common tradition that the thirteenth of the fifth month was the day on which Kuan Chuang-miu (關 壯 繆 i.e., Kuan Ti) crossed the Yangtse Kiang to attend an assembly in the State of Wu. So if there is rain on this day, it is called " sword-grinding rain."

> *Note*: Kuan Ti, the God of War, who has been one of the most popular deities among the people, (*cf* p. 55), especially during the Manchu dynasty, is the deified Kuan Yü 關 羽 who died A.D. 219. He was one of the three famed " sworn brothers " who fought heroically against their opponents during the period of China's chivalry which brought to an end the Later Han dynasty and ushered in the period of the Three Kingdoms. The incident here referred to is that in which in A.D. 215 he was treacherously invited across the river to a banquet given by Sun Ch'üan, leader of the rival State of Wu. He went there alone, having first ground his sword sharp, and escaped assassination only through his great courage.

DIVIDING THE DRAGON HOSTS (*Fen Lung Ping* 分 龍 兵)

Pekinese call the twenty-third day of the fifth month that of the dividing of the dragon hosts. This is because the time from the fifth month onward is that of the big rains, when there is likely to be rain on the adjoining cart rut (while none has fallen on the one beside it). (It is believed that) this must therefore be due to a division made among the dragon hosts.

According to what the *P'i Ya*, by Liu Tien of the Sung dynasty, says, the fifth month was then commonly called the time of the rain of the divided dragons. When someone would speak of " rain of the adjoining cart rut " (*ko ch'e yü* 隔 轍 雨) he had reference to the

---

[1] *Ta han pu kuo wu yüeh shih san* 大 旱 不 過 五 月 十 三.

KUAN TI, THE GOD OF WAR

Rubbing from a stone tablet

extreme difference in rainfall (which may occur during the season of summer rains between one place and the area adjoining it). For each dragon has his own territory parcelled out to him (within which he has complete control over the rainfall), so that rain and clear weather are constantly being differentiated by merely the space between two adjoining cart ruts.

From this we can see that the talk about the division of dragons is already to be found in Sung times, only the designated day being different. In Sung times it was said that the twentieth day of the fourth month was that of the small dividing of dragons, and the twentieth day of the fifth month was that of the big division. When great clearness prevailed on these days there would be drought; when much rain, inundation.

MONTH OF EVIL (Ô Yüeh 惡 月)

A Peking proverb says: " The first month is good; the fifth month evil." [1]

According to the *Ching-ch'u Sui-shih-chi*, the fifth month was then commonly called the evil month, during which month there were many things to be avoided. Hence one should avoid airing beds or mats in the sun, or repairing or building a house. Thus we can see that even though the State of Ching, that is of Ch'u,[2] was far removed from Yen Ching (an ancient name for Peking), all the same from of old there have been points of identity in their customs.

POMEGRANATES AND OLEANDERS

In Peking the fifth month is precisely the time when the pomegranates come into flower, so that their fresh luster dazzles the eyes. Householders all have them arranged in their courtyard together with oleanders, so as to have something fresh to enjoy. Between the pomegranates and the oleanders there must always be a large earthenware fish-jar arranged in a symmetrical way, with several goldfish swimming inside. In practically every house it is like this, so that

---

[1] *Shan cheng yüeh, ó wu yüeh* 善 正 月 惡 五 月 .
[2] *Cf.* Note on p. 42.

there is a Peking proverb which speaks of " a mat covering overhead, an earthenware fish-jar, and a pomegranate tree,"[1] thus mocking at their uniformity.

FIFTH MONTH FIRSTS (*Wu Yüeh Hsien-er* 五 月 先 兒)

In the fifth month when the corn (called " jade grain " or *yü mi* 玉 米) first comes into seed, the streets are filled with the shouts of vendors calling : " Fifth month firsts ! " And of the extremely tender ones they cry : " Precious pearl shoots ! " The way of eating them is the same as that for eating peas.

SWEET MELONS

By the last decade (twenty-first to twenty-ninth or thirtieth) of the fifth month the sweet melons have already become ripe. The street vendors who shout their wares have every kind, such as " dry golden droppers," " green-skin crushables," " sheep-horn honey," " Hami[2] crisps," " Wei[3] pulps," and " old man's delight."

DYEING OF FINGER NAILS

The Chinese balsam is the same as the " penetrating-to-the-bones grass " (*t'ou ku ts'ao* 透 骨 草), and is also called " finger-nail grass " (*chih chia ts'ao* 指 甲 草). In the fifth month when its flower opens, girls collect and pound it so as to dye the finger nails. Its fresh redness " penetrates to the bones, " and will last a year before disappearing.

---

[1] *T'ien p'eng, yü kang, shih liu shu* 天 篷 魚 缸 石 榴 樹
[2], [3] Both places in Chinese Turkestan.

CHAPTER VI—THE SIXTH MONTH

SIXTH DAY OF SIXTH MONTH

ON the sixth day of the sixth month Pekinese shake out and sun their clothes and books, saying that thus insects and bookworms will not appear.[1]

WASHING THE ELEPHANTS

During the time when the elephant stables still contained elephants, the elephants on the sixth day of the sixth month used to be led outside Hsüan Wu Men and into the moat to be washed, at which time spectators would stand lined-up like a wall. But later, because one elephant went mad and injured a man, they were no longer kept. Before the tenth year of Kuang Hsü (1884), however, they were still to be seen.

The elephant stables are inside Hsüan Wu Men, following the city wall westward, and were under the control of the Imperial Equipage Department. When spectators would enter, the elephants could make a sound through their trunks as of conch shells. And when the on-lookers laid down some copper coins, the elephant keeper would make the elephants do tricks at his commands, they looking at him sidewise the while. Only after the full number of copper coins had been received, would they raise their trunks, incline their heads, and let forth a sound.

If they were ill, oil would flow from their ears, and this was said to be the coming forth of their mountain natures. The elephant has a very long span of life, and during the reign of Tao Kuang (1821-1850) there was an old elephant, the tusks of which had a bronze casing, which was said to date from the T'ang dynasty, having been brought by the followers of An (Lu-shan) and Shih (Ssŭ-ming).[2]

---

[1] *Cf.* also the airing of the Buddhist sūtras on this day at Chieh T'ai Ssŭ, pp. 32-34.

[2] 安祿山 and 史思明, two notable rebels whose revolts did much to weaken the T'ang dynasty. That of An Lu-shan lasted from 755 until his death in 757, and that of Shih Ssŭ-ming from 759 until his death in 761.

BRINGING TRIBUTE ELEPHANTS TO PEKING

Later, because the elephant keepers, etc., took too big a " squeeze " from the animals' rations, the elephants one after another died, so that during the ten odd years after Hsien Feng (reigned 1851-1861) the elephant stables were without elephants. But in the last year of T'ung Chih (1874) and first year of Kuang Hsü (1875), Annam twice sent as tribute a total of six or seven elephants which were very fat and sturdy. Spectators used to delight in their peaceful appearance, and rejoiced as they passed along the road. But after the incident of the injured man at Tung Ch'ang An Men,[1] their every movement was prohibited, and they did not again serve the Emperor. Within two or three years all of them had died from starvation.

---

[1] This is the incident of 1884 mentioned above, when one of the elephants used in the royal procession which was returning from the worship at the Altar of Heaven, went amok and injured a man who happened to be near.

According to the *Jih-hsia*, the elephant stables were built in the eighth year of Hung Chih (1495). When the elephants arrived at the Capital, they would first be trained at the place where archery took place, and which was therefore called the place for training elephants. The Imperial Guard had likewise a place for taming elephants, and expressly delegated an Imperial Guard Director for the special super-vision of the elephants and their keepers. At all the great Court functions many elephants would be used to draw chariots and carry precious things, but for ordinary Court affairs only six would be used. The revenue received for their upkeep was graded on a scale similar to that of the military officials. The present dynasty has followed this system as before, only changing the supervision from that of the Imperial Guard to the Imperial Equipage Department.

Worship of the ' God of Horses ' (*Ma Wang* 馬 王)

The Horse God is the constellation of the Room (*Fang* 房, consisting of four stars nearly in a straight line, viz., Beta, Delta, Pi, and Nu, in the head of Scorpio). All military men and people in families which keep carriages and horses, worship him on the twenty-third day of the sixth month.

Worship of the ' God of War ' (*Kuan Ti* 關 帝)

On the twenty-fourth day of the sixth month, every year without fail, worship is rendered to Kuan Ti, when the large number of fire-crackers is no less than on New Year's Day. This is because the god, in opposing disasters and warding off of calamities, brings great benficence to the people.

Imperial Distribution of Ice

In the Capital, beginning from the *shu fu* 暑 伏 days,[1] and lasting until the Beginning of Autumn (*Li Ch'iu*), all the yamens according to custom receive Imperial distribution of ice. At the approach of this season ice tickets are distributed from the Ministry of Works,

---

[1] The period of greatest heat, which begins on the third *keng* 庚 day after the Summer Solstice (*Hsia Chih*, i.e., June 22), and is divided into three periods : the first *fu* of ten days ; the second *fu* of twenty days ; and the last *fu* of an indeterminate number of less than ten days.

which each yamen goes to get for itself. The amount of ice given is not the same, each yamen being graded.

According to the *Ti-ching Ching-wu-lüeh*, during the Ming dynasty the distribution of ice commenced at the Beginning of Summer (*Li Hsia*), when it was given out to the great civil and military officials.

The ice pedlars for the common people hold two brass cups in their hands which they strike together (like castanets) with a continuous clinking. These are called ice cups, and are still found to-day. The clear coldness of the ice may be heard even in their sound, and is indeed a sound suggestive of calm and peace.

CHANGING TO SILK CRÊPE CLOTHES

Every year during the sixth month, lasting from the *shu fu* days until the end of the *shu* period, the various officials all wear yellow silk gauze hats and gowns of yellow silk crêpe.

CENTRAL PEAK (*Chung Ting* 中 項)

The Temple of the Princess of the Colored Clouds at the Central Peak is ten *li* outside Yu An Men at Grass Bridge (Ts'ao Ch'iao). Every year on the first day of the sixth month there is a temple fair, at which are exhibited many flowers and fruit trees, lustrous like embroidery on display. Many men and women of the south city go there to look on.

According to the *Ch'en-yüan Shih-lüeh*, Grass Bridge is ten *li* outside Yu An Men, at a place where several streams come together. Such persons as those who plant things that need irrigation, depend on this fact to help them, for being close to springs, the ground is propitious for flowers. The people who stay here make their living by rearing flowers, and have ponds of lotus whose fragrance may be smelled for several *li*, while peonies of both the big and small varieties are planted like paddy or hemp.

The bridge is ten *li* from Feng T'ai, and during Yüan and Ming times the gardens of many noble families, such as the Hall of Ten Thousand Willows of the Junior Councillor Lien, and the Gourd Pavilion of the Chief of Staff Chao, were all to the left and right of the bridge. But now there is no longer any evidence of all this. . . . .

LAKE OF TEN TEMPLES (*Shih Ch'a Hai* 十刹海)

Note: This lake, which is the continuation northward of the North Lake or Pei Hai, is so called because at one time ten temples lined its banks, though only three of these now remain.

The Shih Ch'a Hai. . . . . is outside Ti An Men, toward the west. Its lotuses are extremely numerous, and every year on the coming of the sixth month men and women assemble here in crowds. But everyone keeps to the north bank of the Front Lake (Ch'ien Hai), and although other places also have lotuses, no one goes to them for enjoyment. The part lying west of the Bridge of Righteous Victory (Te Sheng Ch'iao) is called the Heaped-up Waters Pool (Chi Shui T'an), and is also called the Lake of Pure Learning (Ching Yeh Hu) [1]. . . . .

---

[1] This is the most western and northern division of the lake, just inside Te Sheng Men. Its latter name is derived from a Buddhist temple of the same name on the banks. The next few lines of text are omitted because they give a complicated description of the region, filled with many names, for which the reader would do better to consult Arlington and Lewisohn's *In Search of Old Peking*.

At the time when flowers are blossoming, the scenery along the northern bank section is most lovely. The green willows droop their streamers, women appear with bright colored costumes and brilliant cosmetics, and the flowers shine in people's faces, now concealed and now indistinctly apparent, until one knows not whether it is the people who are people, or the flowers which are flowers [1] . . . . .

GIRL WHO SWEEPS CLEAR THE WEATHER (*Sao Ch'ing Niang* 掃 晴 娘)

The sixth month is the season of great rains, and whenever an unceasing and continuous stretch of wet weather is encountered, the little girls in the women's quarters cut a human figure out of paper and hang it up on the left of the gate, calling it the "girl who will sweep clear the weather." [2]

ICE SEEDS (*Ping Hu-er* 冰 胡 兒)

From the *shu fu* heat period onward, boys of poor families go about Peking carrying ice, which they sell shouting : " Ping hu-er ! " The word *hu* means a seed (i.e., a small lump of ice).

SOUR PRUNE DRINK (*Suan Mei T'ang* 酸 梅 湯)

Sour prune drink or "soup" is made from sour prunes boiled with sugar, to which rose blossoms and olives are added, and is cooled with ice water until it chills the teeth. The Nine Dragon Studio (Chiu Lung Chai) at Ch'ien Men and the House of Ch'iu (Ch'iu Chia) at Hsi Tan P'ailou are most noted for it in the Capital.

WATER-MELONS

By the time of the first decade (first to tenth) of the sixth month, the water-melons have already matured. Among them are such varieties as the "three whites" (skin, pulp and seeds all white), black skin, yellow pulp, and red pulp. They are sold on the streets cut up like lotus petals (i.e., in slices) or like a camel's back (i.e., halved). They come with the heat, and may be eaten on the spot. They purify one from the effects of heat, and can also help one to get over intoxication, so that I have therefore always proclaimed them a purifying and cooling refreshment.

---

[1] Our author continues with a passage from the *Jih-hsia*, giving a list of former names for this region, which is omitted here as being probably of little interest to westerners.

[2] She is the Goddess of the Star of the Broom (*Sao Chou* 掃 箒).

CHAPTER VII—THE SEVENTH MONTH

LAYING DOWN OF NEEDLES (*Tiu Chen* 丟 針)

ON the seventh day of the seventh month girls of Peking each take a bowl of water which they expose to the sun, and put in it a small needle so that it will float on the surface of the water. They then long watch the needle's shadow at the bottom of the water. Sometimes it is diffused as if in the shape of flowers, sometimes in movement like clouds, sometimes fine like a thread, or sometimes thick like a stick. By this means they can predict each girl's dexterity or clumsiness.[1] This is commonly called the laying down of needles.

BRIDGE FORMED OF MAGPIES

On the seventh day of the seventh month, if the morning is clear, the crows and magpies appear flying and calling a little later than usual, and it is commonly said that they have been away forming a bridge.

Note : This has reference to an old legend, according to which the celestial Spinning Damsel (identified with the constellation Lyra) was banished from Heaven for a certain period and sent to earth. There she met the Oxherd (identified with the constellation Aquila), whom she married. They lived happily together until the time when her banishment came to an end, when she was forced to return to Heaven. The Oxherd tried to pursue her, only to be stopped in his progress by the Heavenly River (Milky Way), and since that time the lovers have been permitted to see each other only once a year, on the seventh day of the seventh month, when the magpies are supposed to form a bridge across the Milky Way over which the two may pass. But if on that day it rains, they are doomed to wait another year before meeting. A play representing this lovely legend is usually given on this day.

According to the *Jih-hsia*, during the Chin (1115-1234) and Yüan (1280-1367) dynasties the courtiers of the Palace would wear (embroidered) insignia of a magpie bridge. On the Lantern Festival they would wear ones of lanterns, and on the *Tuan Yang*, insignia of gourds. These were all to mark the occasion of the festival. But the present dynasty, with its august frugality, has not revived such childish forms of amusement.

---

[1] Thus a shadow thick like a stick would indicate that the girl is clumsy at needlework, whereas one fine like a thread would show the reverse.

FIFTEENTH DAY OF SEVENTH MONTH (*Chung Yüan* 中 元)

The *Chung Yüan* is not a festival, but simply a time when sacrifices are made to the ancestors and the ancestral graves are swept.[1]

LANTERNS OF LOTUS-LEAVES, LOTUS-FLOWERS, AND ARTEMISIA

From twilight onward on the *Chung Yüan* day, boys of the streets light lanterns made out of lotus leaves (in the deep hollow of which

LANTERNS OF LOTUS-LEAVES AND LOTUS-FLOWERS

they stick a candle, so that it makes a beautiful glow through the green leaf), and go along the streets singing :

"Lotus-leaf candles ! Lotus-leaf candles !
To-day you are lighted. To-morrow thrown away ! "[2]

---

[1] This " middle " *Yüan*, like the first or " upper " *Yüan* (the Lantern Festival), comes always at the time of full moon, and is one of the most picturesque of all the Chinese celebrations.

[2] *Ho yeh teng ! Ho yeh teng !* 荷 葉 燈！ 荷 葉 燈！
Chin jih tien liao ! Ming jih jeng ! 今 日 點 了！ 明 日 扔！

Also from green artemisia plants they make (ropes of) glutinous incense and light them, so that they gleam like the innumerable dots of moving fireflies. These are called artemisia lanterns. Ingenious merchants likewise make the forms of lotus blossoms, lotus leaves, flower baskets, herons, and egrets, all cut out of colored paper, calling them all lotus-flower lanterns.

According to the *Jih-hsia*, the making of lotus-leaf lanterns has come down to us from the Yüan and Ming dynasties, so that to-day we still follow an old custom.

'Boat of the Law' (*Fa Ch'uan* 法 船)

On the *Chung Yüan* day each Buddhist temple makes a "boat of the Buddhist law" (out of paper) and burns it in the evening, some being as much as several tens of feet long.

Note: As explained in the next section, the *Chung Yüan* day, though it may have earlier origins, is now primarily a Buddhist festival held to help those spirits who are homeless or who have no descendants who can say masses for them, and especially for the spirits of persons who have been drowned, and who therefore have no resting place. The "boat of the law" is made at this time to help such wandering spirits to cross the sea of want, hunger, thirst, and torment into which their sins had gotten them when they were over-taken by death, and so to enable them to reach Nirvana. This festival, with its masses for the dead, seems to have been made popular by Amogha Vajra (in Chinese, Pu-k'ung Chin-kang 不 空 金 剛), who arrived in China from northern India in A.D. 719, and reached a position of great importance by the time of his death in 772.

All Souls' Day (*Yü Lan Hui* 盂 蘭 會)

On the *Chung Yüan* day each Buddhist temple forms a *Yü Lan* Society (*Hui*) which lights lanterns and recites sūtras so as to lead those deeply engulfed in the lower world (across the sea of suffering).

According to what the Buddhist sūtras say, the Buddha once commanded Mu Lien,[1] because his mother had been reborn among the Hungry Devils (in Hades), where she was not allowed anything to eat, to form a *Yü Lan P'en* Society, which on the fifteenth day of the seventh month would put all kinds of different-tasting fruits into basins, and offer them so as to nurture great virtue in the ten quarters.[2]

---

[1] In Sanskrit, Maudgalyayana, one of Sakyamuni Buddha's disciples.
[2] The eight compass points, and above and below.

And after this his mother would be allowed to eat.[1] Mu Lien replied
to the Buddha that all those disciples who practised filiality and obedience
ought likewise to make *Yü Lan P'en* offerings. The Buddha expressed
great approval of this, and later generations have ever since acted in
accordance with it.

But according to what the *Shih-shih Yao-lan* says, the term *Yü
Lan P'en* is a transcription from the Sanskrit (*Ullambana*), and means
in Chinese, "to be suspended upside down."[2] Hence present-day
people who set out basins (*p'en*, one of the words in the Chinese
transcription) to make offerings with, err (in their interpretation of
the term).

> *Note :* This has for long been a common explanation offered by both Chinese and westerners.
> Przyluski, however, has shown that the term *Yü Lan P'en* is probably not a transcrip-
> tion of the Sanskrit *Ullambana*, but rather of *Avalambana*, a term which seems to have
> been applied in India to certain meritorious offerings made to the whole living
> community, through which benefit might be acquired for the dead. This would
> indicate that this festival has certain Indian origins. *Cf.* his *Les Rites d'Avalambana*,
> in *Mélanges chinois et bouddhiques*, I. p. 221. For a translation and discussion of the
> whole Mu Lien story, see Jan Jaworski, *L'Avalambana sûtra de la terre pure*, in
> *Monumenta Serica*, Vol. I, No. 1, pp. 82-107.

SETTING OUT OF RIVER LANTERNS

There are many people who from the *Tuan Yang* festival onward,
come to the Second Sluice on the Grand Canal (Yün Ho) for recreation.
And on the *Chung Yüan* day there is customarily a *Yü Lan* Society,
members of which perform various entertainments such as stilt
walking, or dressing themselves up as lions (to do lion-dances).
During the evening lanterns are lighted along the canal, this being
called the "setting out of river lanterns."

> *Note :* Hundreds of small candles fastened to floats are set adrift on the waters, again to guide
> the spirits of those who have been drowned, while adults and children walk along the
> banks carrying the beautiful lotus-leaf lanterns described above. Many people come
> on this evening to witness this, one of the most beautiful of Chinese festivals.[3]

TEMPLE OF CITY GOD FROM SOUTH OF THE YANGTSE KIANG
(*Chiang Nan Ch'eng Huang Miao* 江 南 城 隍 廟)

The Chiang Nan Ch'eng Huang Miao is outside Cheng Yang Men,
at the east end of Nan Heng Chieh, north-west of the Altar of Agriculture.

---

[1] Once during her lifetime she had unwittingly eaten some meat, and later when accused of the
deed had angrily denied it, in consequence of which she was dragged off to Hades.

[2] *Tao hsüan* 倒 懸, that is, it refers to the state of suffering of lost spirits, to relieve whom the
masses given for the dead at this time are recited.

[3] We omit the following section, giving a detailed description of the canal which links Peking

It was founded under K'ang Hsi (1662-1722), and inside it is a rest-room for the City Gods (from China south of the Yangtse). Every year on *Chung Yüan*, as well as on *Ch'ing Ming* and on the first day of the tenth month, it has a temple fair, when the people of the Capital welcome and give offerings to these lonely gods. . . . .

Note : This temple was established as a place where the many persons in Peking from the south of China might offer sacrifice to and seek aid from their own local tutelary deities.

'LITTLE GOLDEN BELL' CRICKETS (*Chin Chung-er* 金鐘兒)

The "little golden bell" crickets (*homeogryllus japonicus*) breed in I Chou (the district in which the Western Imperial Tombs or Hsi Ling are located). They are like the (usual) cricket in shape, and are transported to Peking for sale in the latter part of the seventh month. When one listens to them while lying in bed, their chirp is surpassingly clear, musical but not sad, as if they were born to be creatures of large rooms and lofty halls (i.e., of noble homes). Surely their title of " golden bell " has not been one extravagantly conferred on them.

WATER-CHESTNUTS AND 'CHICKEN-HEAD' SEEDS

By the time of the middle decade (eleventh to twentieth) of the seventh month the water-chestnuts and *chi t'ou*[1] have come up, so that the pedlars shout along the streets : " Old chicken heads ! Just out of the river ! " Both of these are products from the Imperial waterways.

DATES AND GRAPES

By the time of the last decade (twentieth to twenty-ninth or thirtieth) of the seventh month the dates hang down in their redness and the grapes have become purple. Those who carry them about on poles slung over their shoulders, always sell them together, and when the autumn sound of their cry enters the ears, its musical note gives a suggestion of chilliness and a sad melancholy. Indeed there is no way of preventing one from feeling the emotions that go with the seasons of the year.

---

and the little town of T'ung Chou, about forty *li* to the east, where it joins the terminus of the Grand Canal, over which in the old days rice from the south was transported to the Capital.

[1] 雞 頭 : *eurayle ferox*, a water plant the seeds of which are edible, and are called " chicken heads " from the appearance of the pods.

CHAPTER VIII—THE EIGHTH MONTH

'MID-AUTUMN' FESTIVAL (*Chung Ch'iu* 中 秋)

PEKINESE call the festival of the eighth month the *Chung Ch'iu*, and every year at this time noble families make presents to one another of moon cakes (*yüeh ping* 月 餅) and various fruits. This, the fifteenth day, is the time when the moon is full, and so melons and fruits are laid out in the courtyard as offerings to her. Sacrifices are also made with yellow beans (intended for the rabbit in the moon), and cockscomb flowers (the flower of this month). At this time the white disk of the moon hangs in the void, and when the tinted clouds first begin to scatter, winecups are arranged and bowls washed amidst the noisy hubbub of the children. Verily it is what one may call a beautiful festival. However, at this time of making offerings to the moon, men usually do not make any obeisances, so that there is a Peking proverb which says : " Men do not bow to the moon. Women do not sacrifice to the God of the Kitchen." [1]

Note : This is because the moon is supposed to belong to the *yin* or female principle, just as the sun is male or *yang*. Therefore it would be inappropriate for a man to worship the moon, whereas as the head of the household he would naturally sacrifice to the God of the Kitchen. *Cf.* p. 98.

MOON EFFIGIES (*Yüeh Kuang Ma-er* 月 光 馬 兒)

Pekinese call the effigy of a deity, the deity's *ma-er*, not daring to speak directly of it itself as a deity. Moon effigies (*yüeh kuang ma-er*) are made out of paper, on the upper part of which is painted the Goddess of the Moon (T'ai Yin Hsing Chün 太 陰 星 君), having the form of a Bodhisattva.[2] Below is painted the " palace of the moon " (*yüeh kung* 月 宮, i.e., the moon's disk), with the jade rabbit

---

[1] *Nan pu pai yüeh, nü pu chi tsao* 男 不 拜 月，女 不 祭 灶.

[2] A Bodhisattva is a Mahayana Buddhist saint who refuses to become a Buddha and enter Nirvana until all other living beings in the universe have been saved. The Goddess of the Moon is Ch'ang Ô 嫦 娥, who fled to the moon after stealing from her husband, the noted archer, Hou I 后 羿, the elixir of immortality. Her husband later became the God of the Sun, and the two are said to meet once a month at the time of new moon.

who pounds drugs, standing like a man and holding a pestle.[1] The drug's colors and the essence made from it are of a gold iridescent brilliancy.

Many shops sell such objects, of which the tall ones may be seven or eight feet high, whereas short ones are only two or three feet. On their tops are two pennants (one at each corner) which are made red, blue, or yellow. One places them facing the moon and offers them, at the same time burning incense and making obeisances. When the sacrifice is finished, they are all burned, together with such things as " thousand sheets " (*ch'ien chang* 千 張) and *yüan pao* (元 寶)......

Note : These are both forms of " spirit money," that is, imitation paper money to be burned for the dead. The first is cut out in the form of a series of connected zigzag strips (the "thousand sheets"), while the second is shaped like a shoe of silver sycee. [Ferguson]

NINE-JOINTED LOTUS ROOTS

When members of the Court make their moon offerings, according to custom they use nine-sectioned lotus roots.

Note : The lotus, rising as it does from the slime of ponds to become a thing of beauty, is the Buddhist emblem of purity, and hence its various parts are thought to purify the body of noxious poisons and evil conditions. Its root, which forms a food much relished by the Chinese, never by itself grows to more than three or four joints. But out of several sections cleverly spliced together, one long root can be made having nine joints, the lucky number.

' LOTUS PETAL ' WATER-MELONS

At all *Chung Ch'iu* moon offerings there should be water-melons cut out irregularly in the shape of the petals of a lotus.

MOON CAKES (*Yüeh Ping* 月 餅)

For the *Chung Ch'iu* moon cakes, the Studio of Perfect Beauty (Chih Mei Chai, a shop) at Ch'ien Men, is the best place in the Capital, whereas those of other places are not worth eating. But as for moon cakes to be used solely as moon offerings, every shop has them. The big ones are more than a foot in diameter, and have portrayed on their

---

[1] The moon is inhabited, according to Taoist conception, by such a rabbit, who is forever busy pounding up the elixir of life.

tops the images of the three-legged toad and the rabbit of the moon.[1] Some people eat these cakes as soon as the sacrifices to the moon are completed, whereas other people keep them until New Year's Eve before eating them.   They are called full moon cakes (*t'uan yüan ping* 團 圓 餅).

> *Note* :   These cakes are of early origin, but the little paper squares stuck on them, according to a story, not found, however, in the orthodox histories, go back to the latter part of the Yüan dynasty.   At this time the Chinese were very closely watched by their Mongol overlords.   Mongol spies were stationed in private families ; people were not permitted to gather into groups for conversation ; and no weapons were permitted, even vegetable and meat choppers being restricted to one for every ten families.   Finally, according to the story, someone conceived the idea of attaching papers to the moon cakes which are universally sent to one's friends at this festival, and of writing thereon a message for uprising.   The resulting midnight massacre of Mongols led to the ultimate overthrow of the dynasty.

According to the *Ti-ching Ching-wu-lüeh*, the fifteenth day of the eighth month was then that of sacrifice to the moon.   The fruits and cakes used in this sacrifice had to be round (like the full moon), and the melons must be irregularly toothed, cut out like the petals of a lotus.   Stationery shops at this time would sell " moon papers " (*yüeh-kuang chih* 月 光 紙, i.e., the " moon effigies " described above) on which were portrayed a full moon and, sitting cross-legged, a Bodhisattva whom the moonlight would completely illuminate. Beneath all this glory, in the moon's disk, would be the hall of the cassia tree,[2] in which was a rabbit with a pestle, who stood like a man, pounding drugs in a mortar. . . . .

Families would set up these " moon nimbuses " in the direction where the real moon comes up, and make offerings and bow down while facing the moon.   Then they would burn the paper moon nimbus and remove what had been offered, distributing it without exception to everyone in the house.   Relatives gave moon cakes and fruits to one another, the cakes having a diameter of two feet. Married women who had been making visits to their parents had to return to their husbands' homes on this day. . . . .

---

[1] This toad, like the jade rabbit, is also an inhabitant of the moon, and some legends say that he is really the Goddess of the Moon, Ch'ang O, who was transformed into a toad.

[2] This cassia tree, and a woodcutter, not mentioned here, who is forever engaged in chopping it down, are still other creatures of the moon.   But his is a vain task indeed, for as rapidly as he chops it down, this tree, which is a giver of life to others, miraculously repairs its own injuries.

What is quoted in the last passage is for the greater part identical with what occurs to-day, so that we can see how far back go the references to moon offerings.

T'U-ER YEH, THE RABBIT
Dressed up as a general with attendants.

RABBIT IMAGES

Every year on the *Chung Ch'iu*, ingenious merchants model images out of clay of the three-legged toad and the rabbit, to be put out for sale. These latter are called "gentleman rabbits" (*t'u-er yeh* 兔兒爺). Some are dressed in gown and bonnet, with an outstretched umbrella; some wear armor and helmet and carry a large military flag; and some ride tigers while others sit quietly. The big ones are three feet high and the small ones somewhat over a foot. Over and above the few kinds here described, there is no possible fine variety that is not prepared by the artisans. These are all simply for having fun.

TEMPLE OF THE GOD OF THE KITCHEN (*Tsao Chün Miao* 皂君廟)

The Tsao Chün Miao is outside Ch'ung Wen Men, and is opened for three days each year, beginning from the first day of the eighth month. For this is the birthday of the God of the Kitchen.[1]

---

[1] For this god, *cf.* p. 98. Cooks particularly frequent the temple at this time, because the God of the Kitchen is their patron deity.

CHAPTER IX—THE NINTH MONTH

NINTH DAY OF NINTH MONTH

THE ninth day of the ninth month is called in Peking the Double Yang (*Ch'ung Yang* 重 陽).[1] On this day people of the Capital take a kettle and winecups, and go out to the suburbs to climb some high spot. In the south they go to such places as the Temple of Heavenly Peace (T'ien Ning Ssŭ), Joyful Pavilion (T'ao Jan T'ing), and the Dragon-Claw Locust Tree (Lung Chao Huai). In the north are such places as the Density of Trees Surrounding the Gate of Chi (Chi Men Yen Shu) and the Wall of Pure Metamorphosis (Ch'ing Ching Hua Ch'eng). Farther away are the Eight Buddhist Temples in the Western Hills (i.e., Pa Ta Ch'u). Reciting poetry and drinking wine, roasting meat and distributing cakes—truly this is a time of joy.

Note : There is a legend to explain this hill-climbing ceremony, according to which during the Later Han dynasty (A.D. 25-220) there lived a certain Fei Ch'ang-fang, noted for his knowledge of the magical arts, who had a friend named Huan Ching. One day Fei said to Huan : " On the ninth day of the ninth month a great disaster will happen in your family. But if you have the members of your family make a sack for you out of red silk gauze, fill it with dogwood, and bind it on your arm ; and if you all climb to a high place and drink wine of chrysanthemums (which are supposed to have special life-giving properties because their appearance is suggestive of the sun), the calamity may be lessened." Huan Ching followed this advice, and on returning on the evening of the ninth day, found that his oxen, sheep, chickens, and dogs had all suffered a violent death. Thereupon Fei told him : " They have suffered the disaster which would have befallen you." [2]

FISHING TERRACE (*Tiao Yü T'ai* 釣 魚 臺)

The Fishing Terrace is about three *li* outside Fou Ch'eng Men and has an (Imperial) rest-room facing the south. Every year on *Ch'ung Yang* day many young people of the Capital race here. It is commonly called the Hall Overlooking the Waters (Wang Hai Lou).

---

[1] The number nine is used to designate the unbroken, that is the *yang* or male, lines in the hexagrams of the *I Ching* (Book of Changes), which is the reason why the ninth day of the ninth month should be called the Double *Yang*.

[2] Our author follows the preceding paragraph with quotations from the *Jih-hsia*, giving the history of the various spots mentioned above, but as these are already described in other books on Peking, such as Arlington and Lewisohn's *In Search of Old Peking*, we will not repeat them here.

According to the *Jih-hsia*, the Fishing Terrace is about one *li* north-west of Three *Li* River (San Li Ho), and was a place frequented by the Chin dynasty (1115-1234) rulers. In front of the terrace is a spring which gushes forth from the ground, never ceasing winter or summer. All the little streams flowing from the foot of the Western Hills collect into one here. During the Yüan dynasty it was called the Pool of Jade Depths (Yü Yüan T'an), being then a pool in the garden of the Ting family, while during the present dynasty, in the twenty-eighth year of Ch'ien Lung (1763), it was dug out into a lake so as to receive the waters of the newly opened stream led here from the Fragrant Mountain (Hsiang Shan, the former Imperial "Hunting Park" in the Western Hills). In addition a sluice was built at its lower outlet so as to allow for increased or decreased flow. The waters of the lake, and those which are led along the stream from San Li Ho, meet the city moat at Fou Ch'eng Men.

In the thirty-ninth year (1774) it was first commanded by Imperial decree to construct the terrace, and the three characters *Tiao Yü T'ai* (literally "hooking-fish terrace") were written by the Emperor (Ch'ien Lung) and put on the west side of the terrace. Therefore whenever an Imperial visit is made to the Hsi Ling, or when the Emperor goes from the gardens (i.e., the Summer Palace or other Imperial pleasure spots in the Western Hills) to sacrifice at the Altar of Heaven (T'ien T'an), he must breakfast at this place. Left of the platform are the Yang Yüan Chai 養源齋 and Hsiao Pi T'ing 瀟碧亭 (a small building and a pavilion) which are both remarkable.

Note: The above description hardly does justice to the lake, which must be somewhat more than a mile long, and the banks of which are lined with beautiful weeping willows, making a splendid place for walks. The horse races used to take place on the road running around the lake. The Fishing Terrace itself, with its crenelated wall, is at the eastern end of the lake, where the canal runs through the sluice, and joins the city moat, not near P'ing Tse Men, as our author says, but nearer to Hsi Pien Men. Now, unfortunately, the lake has dried up and is choked with reeds. The whole place has been taken over by the School of Agriculture of Peiping University.

FLOWER CAKES (*Hua Kao* 花糕)

There are two kinds of flower cakes. One of these is made of sugar and flour, with pressed dainty fruits inside, and may be in two or three layers. This is the best kind of flower cake. The other is a steamed cake, the top of which is dotted with dates and prunes, this being a cake of the second grade. Every year at the *Ch'ung Yang* time the shops make these to be used at this festival.

According to the *Hsi-ching-chih*, the people of the Capital would make cakes on the ninth day of the ninth month out of flour and give presents of them at the occasion of the *Ch'ung Yang* festival. Also they would be shouted and vended along the streets in bamboo baskets, in the same way as today. Again, according to the *Ti-ching Ching-wu-lüeh*, there used to be wheat-flour cakes, the surface of which was sprinkled with dates and prunes, called flower cakes. Cake shops would advertise these with a blue flag, and fathers and mothers would invite their married daughters to come to eat them (at the parental home), this being called the "festival for daughters" (*nü-er chieh* 女兒節).

But cake shops to-day do not have advertising flags, nor is there any of this inviting of the daughter to come home and eat. This goes to show the differences in the customs.

CHRYSANTHEMUM HILLOCKS (*Chiu Hua Shan-tzŭ* 九花山子)

The chrysanthemum (*chü* 菊) is also called the "nine flower" (because it flowers during the ninth month). At every coming of the *Ch'ung Yang* festival rich and noble families take several hundred pots of chrysanthemums and place them on a framework high in front and low in the rear, in the middle of a large room, so that they look like a hill. These are called "chrysanthemum hillocks," while when the four sides are raised to a point, they are called "chrysanthemum pagodas" (*chiu hua t'a* 九花塔) . . . . .

Peking's varieties of chrysanthemums are extremely numerous. They are divided into stalks of last year and stalks of this year, coarse stalks and fine stalks. Among last year's stalks of the fine variety are the "honey linked-bracelets," "silver-red needle," "peach-blossom fan," "square golden seal," "eyebrows of the Old Ruler" (i.e., the Taoist sage, Lao Tzŭ), "radiant beauty of Hsi Shih" (a famous beauty of the fifth century B.C.), "concubine of the Hsiao and Hsiang Rivers,"

" goose-quills," " rice-gold duct," " lamp-wick duct," " purple tiger-whiskers," " ash-crane wings," " wild goose settling on level sand," " spring swallow in an apricot orchard," " white softness facing the south," " gold unadorned," " snow-covered azure mountain," " snow-covered cinnabar," " white crane sleeping in the snow," " azure lotus," " azure water-lily," " red-petalled," " Hsiang River lotus," " jade pool," " peach-red," " jade shoots," " long jade hall," " precious monastery of the spring dawn," " Buddhist red," " clay-speckled gold," " speckled lotus-root color," " rainbow-skirted," " egg-plant blue, " and " priest's robe."

Among last year's stalks of the coarse variety are the " big red precious pearl," " gold linked-bracelets," " gold mist bracelets," " great golden sunflower," " dripping-gold sunflower," " golden plate presenting dew," [1] " golden-hair lion," " golden phœnix wings," " outstretched wings of purple phœnix," " purple dragon with opened claws," " purple crab claws," " purple of the Hsü family," " yellow crane feathers," " egret-crane feathers," " azure dragon-whiskers," " azure dragon teaching his son," " lustrous variegated cloud-dragon," " two-colored lotus," " lily on a dazzling day," " dry-land golden lotus" (i.e., Chinese woman's bound feet), " autumn beauty of the hibiscus," " jade fan," " silver needle," " purple pine-needle," " jade spoon stirring broth," " decorated screen," " white peony," " purple peony," " variegated peony," " starlight in the water," " radiance falling from a maple forest " (i.e., maple leaves falling in autumn ?), " oblique light of the evening sun," " evening sun on a duck's back," " blue of mist at break of day," and " blue winged nine."

Among this year's stalks of the fine variety are the " silver tiger-whiskers," " black tiger-whiskers," " red-and-black double radiance," " cinnabar rolled up in gold," " golden phœnix holding a pearl in its mouth," " spring dawn at the Han palace," " flowers washed at a brook," " half-water half-sky," " red mist," " clear mist on autumn waters," " hibiscus of autumn waters," " two proud persons vying in

---

[1] Dew is considered to have magical life-giving properties, since it is supposed to be the congealed essence of the moon, which belongs to the *yin* or female principle. Hence plates were formerly set out at night to collect the dew, and in the Pei Hai park, on the north slope of the hill behind the dagoba, may still be seen a large standing bronze figure holding aloft such a dew-plate.

beauty," " Heavenly Maid (i.e., Spinning Maiden) scattering flowers,"
" peach blossom with a human face," " bird's talon Immortal," " yellow
crane Immortal," " official in lamb's fur," " Immortal's palms,"
" intoxicated T'ai Po," [1] " Ancient Immortal of the south pole,"
" phœnix flute," " *luan* 鸞 bird (a fabulous bird) reed-organ," " ocean
butterfly," " hung-up horns of the antelope," " fragrant white pear,"
" gold as one likes it," " quartzcrystal as one likes it," " yellow
geranium," " red-coral hook," " willow streamers drooping gold,"
and " two suns together."

Among this year's stalks of the coarse variety are the " golden
Buddha seat," " jade suspended from a golden hook," " big red with
golden border," " jade hall with a golden horse," " purple ribbon
and golden seal," " purple jacket and golden belt," " purple lightning
and azure frost," " yellow orioles in the green willows," " intoxicated
Yang Kuei-fei dancing," [2] " Hsi Shih's face powder," " unicorn and
parrot," " embracing a child," " beehive," and " a good time being
had by a united family." [3]

This makes a total of one hundred and thirty-three kinds, all of
which I remember. But for those who can think of them, there are
still more than two hundred other kinds among these four classes.
Some day when I have leisure, I certainly intend to compile a list of
flowers.

FRUITS AND FOODS OF THE SEASON

At the *Ch'ung Yang* festival time, pickled crabs eaten together with
Liang Hsiang wine are very sweet and delicate. Liang Hsiang wine
is produced in the district of Liang Hsiang (which is near Peking,
west of the Marco Polo Bridge or Lu Kou Ch'iao), but in recent times
Peking itself has also been able to make it. Its taste is pure and rich,
and when one drinks it one has a feeling of well-being. It only fears
the heat, so that it cannot pass through the summer. " Duckling

---

[1] Li T'ai Po 李 太 白 (705 ?-762) is China's greatest poet, and was also noted for his fondness
of the bottle, under whose influence many of his most divine poems were written.

[2] *Cf.* Note on p. 41.

[3] A few terms, so recondite as to be very difficult to translate into English, have been left untranslated. Names of this sort are extremely difficult to put into English, and the translator hopes
for the indulgence of his readers for any slips he may have committed.

yellows " are a kind of pear, shaped like a quince, and like the yellow of ducklings in color. . . . . Persimmons and red hawthorns have uses even more numerous and are both Peking products of the season.

According to the *Chi-yüan-chi-so-chi*, during the time when T'ai Tsu (1368-1398), founder of the Ming dynasty, was still obscure, he was once passing through Sheng Ch'ai Ts'un, having already gone two days without food. Walking slowly alone, he reached a place which had once been some family's garden. But now the wall was gone and the trees were hacked down, having been cut up for the fires of soldiers. His Majesty gave a sigh of sorrow, and paced slowly, looking about him the while. In the north-east corner was a single tree, the frost-bitten persimmons on which were just ripe. His Majesty took some and ate them, consuming ten until he reached repletion. Then, after yet grieving a long time, he went away.

In the summer of the *Yi-wei* year (1355), when he seized T'ai P'ing Lu (the present Tang T'u district in Anhuei) by means of Ts'ai Shih (a place twenty *li* north-west of Tang T'u), he passed here again, and found the tree still standing. His Majesty pointed it out, and described to his followers what had once taken place. Then he dismounted and wrapped the tree with a red robe, saying : " I hereby invest you with the title, ' Marquis of Ice and Frost.' "

This was indeed a persimmon tree able to be of service to a ruler of men ! And why then should the record of it be more fragmentary than the records of other things ? For to have met this persimmon tree was good fortune indeed.

TEMPLE OF THE GOD OF WEALTH (*Ts'ai Shen Miao* 財 神 廟)

The Ts'ai Shen Miao is outside Chang I Men, and each year beginning from the fifteenth day of the ninth month, the temple is opened for three days. At this time those who go to worship follow one another continuously, actors and sing-song girls being especially numerous. Gentry and officials such as enjoy affairs of this sort, also sometimes order their horses to be harnessed so that they can go and look on [1] . . . . .

---

[1] This temple is near the Race Course, or P'ao Ma Ch'ang, and is also much frequented the second day after New Year. *Cf.* p. 2.

CHAPTER X—THE TENTH MONTH

FIRST DAY OF TENTH MONTH

THE first day of the tenth month is a time when the people of the Capital sacrifice to, and sweep (the graves of, their ancestors). In common speech it is called the " time of sending winter clothes " to the ancestors (*sung han i* 送寒衣).

According to the *Pei-ching Sui-hua-chi*, on the first of the tenth month one would go to the graves of one's ancestors as at the *Chung Yüan* time, and make sacrifice with *tou-ni-ku-to* 豆泥骨朵. But this *tou-ni-ku-to* is speech of the Yüan Mongols, and we do not know to-day what sort of thing it may have been.

Note : Grube, in his *Zur Pekinger Volkskunde*, p. 86, suggests that this was balls of bean curd, but gives no authority for his supposition.

Again, according to the *Ti-ching Ching-wu-lüeh*, stationery shops on the first day of the tenth month would cut out colored paper to make men's and women's suits of clothes, each one foot and some odd inches long, these being called " winter clothes." On them would be inscriptions giving the family name, personal designation, and generation (of the ancestor to whom the clothes were to be sent), just as when one sends a family letter. All families got these ready, and at night they were offered and burned at the gate. This was called the " sending of winter clothes."

At the present time these are substituted for by plain paper wrappers, so that there still exists the name, " winter clothes," but not the reality. These wrappers are used to enclose some spirit-money, as if in a paper envelope, and on them are written the family name, first name, and generation (of the ancestor for whom they are destined), as described above.

LIGHTING OF FIRES

The householders of the Capital start their fires, according to custom, on the first day of the tenth month, and take out these fires on the first day of the second month. The stoves are made of amianthus (a kind of asbestos), whiter than alum, light, warm, and sturdy.

According to the *Hsi-ching-chih*, the inner part of fossils from the Western Hills was called amianthus (*pu-hui-mu* 不 灰 木), from which could be made a sort of coarse cloth, as well as household vessels which would not fear the fire. At that time this mineral was found in the Western Hills.

But the above paragraph is not altogether correct in what it records. That vessels can be made from this material is possible, but I have never seen such a thing as making coarse cloth from it. Perhaps there is a mistake here for asbestos cloth. Moreover this material is actually produced at I Chou, and not in the Western Hills.

DRILL OF TROOPS

The Prospect of Hills and Depressions (Yang Shan Wa) is outside An Ting Men, ten *li* directly north, and has a military platform. Every year on the fifteenth day of the tenth month there is a united drill there by the Eight Banners, who make such manœuvres as the " nine approaches," the " ten linked circles," and a charge at each other by the cavalry of the Commander of the Vanguard Division and the Captain-General of the Guards Division. This has long since become an ordinary custom. In years of great cold there have been cases of soldiers who have frozen to death, so that it is only young and vigorous men who can go to witness the manœuvres.

SALE OF CALENDARS

In the tenth month after the proclamation of the calendar (for the coming year, by the Imperial Board of Astronomy, which each year prepares it and presents it to the Emperor for his approval), big and small book shops put out calendars for sale, while along the streets and lanes pedlars also carry them in boxes on their backs and shout their wares.

Note : These old style calendars, which are as much almanacs as they are calendars, can still be bought to-day at New Year's time, and give an interesting insight into Chinese folklore and fortune-telling. Thus the lunar calendar which I have for the twenty-fifth year of the Republic, announces for New Year's Day (January 24, 1936): " Propitious to make offerings, pray for happiness, ask for posterity, and assemble relatives, friends and scholars " ; for the second day : " Propitious to bathe, shave the head, trim finger and toe nails, cut wood, hunt and fish " ; and for the third day : " Inauspicious for all undertakings." The National Government has tried unsuccessfully to prohibit the printing and sale of these calendars.

KITES, SHUTTLECOCKS, AND OTHER TOYS

Children's toys also have their relationship to the seasons. In Peking from the tenth month onward there are such things as the " æolian harp " (*feng cheng* 風箏) and shuttlecock. The " æolian harp " is another name for the paper kite. Small bamboos are tied to make the frame, which is covered with paper, and made into forms such as that of the flamingo, peacock, large wild goose, and " flying tiger." They are painted with extreme skill, and when children release them into the void, they can indeed make the eyes clearer as one strains to look at them. Some carry æolian harps (small bamboo bows, the strings of which hum in the wind, and which are tied to the

kite), or gongs or drums (which strike in the wind), the sound of which may be heard as they go higher or lower. It is for this reason that they are called " æolian harps."

Shuttlecocks are made of a skin covering, inside of which is a copper coin, with some feathers of the kite bird tied in a tuft on top by a leather cord. When children kick these about, it helps to make their blood circulate and to withstand the cold.

The glass *la-pa* 喇叭 has a mouth like a winecup and a stem two or three feet long. The *pu-pu-teng* 咘咘噔 is like a gourd in shape (i.e., the Chinese gourd, which is shaped like an hour-glass), and has a stem whose length differs

SHUTTLECOCK

GLASS LA-PA

according to whether it is big or small. These (two types of trumpets) are both products of glass factories, and when children puff and blow into them, they serve to bring in pure air.

"Peace drums" (*t'ai p'ing ku* 太平鼓) have an iron circlet above, covered with donkey skin, so that they are like a circular fan in shape, while the handle below is hung with iron rings. When three to five children form a group and beat these with rattan sticks, the booming of the drum above answers to the jingling of the rings below. This drum is also called the "drum which welcomes in the New Year."

The diabolo top is like the wheels of a cart in form, between which is a short axle. Children operate it by jerking two sticks to which is fastened a cotton string (which is given a twist around the central axle, so that the top hums) majestically with a sound like that of a morning bell beyond the horizon.

According to the *Jih-hsia*, kites are traditionally said to have been made by Han Hsin.[1] Also during the Later Han dynasty of the period of the Five Dynasties, Li Yeh[2] made paper kites together with the Emperor Yin Ti (948-950), which they flew outside the Palace gate.

'PEACE DRUM'
Now no longer seen.

---

[1] One of the heroes who rose from obscurity to help Liu Pang, founder of the Han dynasty, to gain the throne. In spite of his services, he later fell under suspicion for treason, and was executed in 196 B.C. I have been unable to find mention of kite-making in his biography, either in *Shih Chi*, Chap. 92, or the *Han Shu*, Chap. 34. But there is an interesting passage in the works of Mo Tzŭ (the famous philosopher who advocated universal love, and who lived 479 ?-381 ? B.C.) which says : "Kung Shu Tzŭ (a famous military engineer of the time) constructed a bird out of bamboo and wood. When it was completed, he flew it, and for three days it did not descend." *Cf.* Y. P. Mei, *Works of Motse*, p. 256. Is this not perhaps an even earlier reference to kites ?

GLASS PU-PU-TENG

Shuttlecocks, having lead or tin as a weight, used to be fashioned from chicken feathers, and when from three to five small children would form a group there would be . . . . [here follows a list of the different manœuvres to be made with the shuttlecock, such as kicking it forwards or backwards, making it sit on the nose, etc.]. This is indeed something that has survived from football.

The glass *la-pa* is not recorded in the *Jih-hsia*. As for the *pu-pu-teng*, it is the same as the "sounding ear-pendant," and was also called the " sounding gourd," or again, " breath led back and forth." Small ones would be three or four inches in diameter ; big ones a foot. They were usually purple in color, and children would blow in and out of them to create a sound.

Again, the *Ti-ching Ching-wu-lüeh* says that on New Year's Day, toward the evening while it is still light, children would beat a drum called the " drum of peace." But we to-day have these as early as the tenth month, and do not wait for them until the evening of New Year's Day. And when this book says that the " peace drum " is the same as the *chieh* 羯 drum, it is in error, for the *chieh* drum is the same as the "bounding drum" used to-day on the stage. It is beaten with two sticks, so that

---

² Li Yeh was a younger brother of the preceding Emperor, Kao Tsu. He liked to make riddles, and organize amusements for the weak Yin Ti. He was also a politician, and died a violent death.

there is a T'ang poem which in reference to it speaks of

" Head like the peak of an azure mountain ;
  Hands like drops of white rain." [1]

If it were a person beating with only one stick, why should the description be so complicated as all this ?

As for the diabolo, the *Jih-hsia* has no record of it.

PACING-HORSE LANTERNS (*Tsou Ma Teng* 走 馬 燈)

" Pacing-horse " lanterns are wheels cut out of paper, so that when they are blown on (by the warm air rising from) a candle (fastened below the wheel), the carts and horses (painted on the paper wheel) move and run round and round without stopping.[2] But when the candle goes out, the whole thing stops. Though this is but a trifling thing, it contains in truth the whole underlying principle of completion and destruction, rise and decay, so that in the thousand ages from antiquity down to to-day, as recorded in the Twenty-four Histories, there is not one which is not like a " pacing-horse " lantern.[3]

Besides this lantern, there are others of such things as carts, sheep, lions, and embroidered balls (so made that they remain lighted even when rolled over the ground). Each year at the coming of the tenth month,[4] such places as Ch'ien Men, Hou Men, Tung Ssŭ P'ailou, and Hsi Tan P'ailou all have them, and for people who have leisure, it is a delightful thing to go leading a child to one of these places, joyfully buy some, and so return.

The " pacing-horse " lamp, with its wheel which is controlled by a flame, and its mechanism revolved by that wheel, is in the same class

---

[1] I.e., both hands constantly beating the drum like drops of rain. The original reads :

T'ou ju ch'ing shan feng, 頭 如 青 山 峰

Shou ju pai yü tien. 手 如 白 雨 點

[2] I.e., the cylinder on which they are painted is made to revolve by the heated air acting on inclined planes.

[3] These Imperial histories give an unbroken record of China's history from the earliest times down through the Ming dynasty. We have here a graphic metaphor of the Chinese concept of history, according to which the history of dynasties and passage of events is ever but an inevitable succession of cyclic rise, maturity, and decay. In the same way while the candle is fresh the " pacing-horse " lantern moves briskly ; but inevitably comes a time when the candle must die and the movement of the lantern ceases.

[4] To-day it would be better to say in the twelfth month, at the approach of New Year.

with the steamships and railroads of the present day. For if its (principle of operation) had been pushed and extended, so that from one abstruse principle there had been a searching further for the next abstruse principle, who knows but that during the last few hundred years there might not have been completed a mechanism of real utility? What a pity that China has so limited herself in the scope of her ingenuity, that for the creations of her brain and the perfected essence of her inventors, she has nothing better to show than a children's toy! In the present day, when others make a step we too must make a step; when others move forward, we too must move forward. If we are amazed at the wonderful powers (of westerners), and remain content

PACING-HORSE LANTERN

in our own stupidity, how can we then say in self-extenuation that the flow of genius produced from the universe should be widespread among them alone, and narrow only among us? Is it not indeed something for which we should be angry with ourselves?

FOOTBALL

From the tenth month onward boys of the poor classes grind stones into small balls, which they kick with their feet backward and forward, the one that strikes the other being the winner. Peking is very cold now, and the toes of one's feet can become frozen. But by keeping up this kicking exercise, boys keep the blood circulating and can ward off the cold. And this in fact is a sort of football.

According to the *Jih-hsia*, football has been in existence from the Chin and Yüan dynasties onward, and thus has not taken its beginning in modern times.

CRICKETS

The cries of insects and birds have a very close connection with the seasons, but wherever man's effort extends, it too is capable of making modifications in the seasons, and hence likewise has a connection with them. In Peking from the fifth month onward, *kua-kua-er*

聒 聒 兒 crickets are sold by street-criers, at which time they do not exceed one or two cash apiece. But in the tenth month when they are reared by artificial heating, they may reach a price of several thousand cash apiece.

In the middle decade (eleventh to twentieth) of the seventh month come the *chü-chü-er* 蛐 蛐 兒, valuable ones of which may cost several taels. Among them are such varieties as those with white-mottled heads, yellow-mottled heads, crab-shell green, *p'i-pa* (琵 琶, a sort of guitar) winged, plum-flower winged, and bamboo-joint whiskers. It is for their capacity to fight (that they are so valued). But by the time of the tenth month they do not exceed a few hundred cash apiece, because they are then only taken for their song (and no longer fight).

In a class with the *chü-chü-er* are the " oily " *hu-lu* (油 壺 盧 i.e., *gryllus mitratus*). For one cash one can buy more than ten of them during the autumn, but by the tenth month they may reach a price of several thousand cash apiece. During their song time, when their chirp now pauses, then continues, vibrating yet prolonged, one may feel both sadness and joy as one listens to it on a winter night. Truly is it a sound appropriate to the man of leisure.

As to the jars made to keep the autumn *chü-chü*, there are such varieties as those of the Imperial pottery of Yung Lo (1403-1424), of Chao Tzŭ-yü 趙 子 玉, of the masters of Tan Yüan 淡 園 and Ching Hsüan 靜 軒, and those made of pure solutions of red and white (clays). A pair of fine ones may cost several tens of taels. Likewise fine gourds for the winter *kua-kua-er* and the " oily " *hu-lu* may also cost several tens of taels a pair. The best are the purple glossy ones which are firm and thick, these being the so-called " gourd vessels." All this is why there are so many impoverished nobles in Peking, and is in fact one reason why the ways in which they squander their riches do not stop merely with music, women, and precious stones.

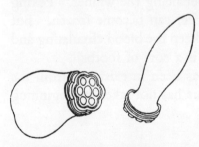

GOURD CRICKET CAGES

According to the *Jih-hsia*, the village of Hu Chia Ts'un, five *li* outside Yung Ting Men, produces good fighting crickets which can overcome crickets produced elsewhere. Stirred by the autumn, they are born. Their sound is that of *shang*,[1] and their nature is that of conquest.

To-day people of the Capital are also able to produce and propagate them, and make their song last long into the winter. The method is to fill a pan with earth, so that the reared insects will give birth to their young in the earth. At the beginning of winter this earth is laid on a warm *k'ang*.[2] This is daily sprinkled with water and is covered with cotton. After standing for five or six days, the eggs begin to wriggle, and after again standing for seven or eight days they become larva. They are given some vegetable leaves, and continue to be sprinkled and covered over.

PING-T'ANG-HU-LU

Their legs and wings now gradually become black, and within a month they sing, even more delicately than in the autumn. They die on the coming of spring. These crickets are called *hsi-shuai* 蟋 蟀, and are divided into three classes: those which are fat and large and have a rich color like oil, which are called " oily " *hu-lu*; those with big heads, called "clothes-beater heads "[3]; and those with sharp jaws, called " old rice mandibles," etc. . . . . [The names of a few other varieties are omitted].

CHESTNUTS, SWEET POTATOES, AND
VARIOUS CANDIES

Peking's foods also have their relationship with the seasons, and from

---

[1] 商, the second note in the Chinese scale of five notes.

[2] 炕, a platform usually made of bricks and built into the room, which is used as a sleeping place, and which in winter can be heated by fire from below.

[3] These clothes-beaters are small thick wooden truncheons used by Chinese women to beat the clothes while washing them.

the tenth month onward there are such things as chestnuts and sweet potatoes. When the chestnuts come, and are roasted with small black pebbles (which prevent them from burning), their sweetness is extraordinarily fine. If one peels and eats a few while pausing from one's reading beneath the lamp, they certainly have a taste beyond compare.

Sweet potatoes are enjoyed by poor and rich alike, and require nothing else but a fire where they may be roasted, being by nature of a fine flavor. In comparison with the potato and taro, they are of greater help to the world (because of their extreme cheapness), and serve at any time as a simple but useful food.

Chung-kuo 中果 and *nan-t'ang* 南糖 candy are to be had anywhere. *Sa-ch'i-ma* 薩齊瑪 are Manchu cakes, and are made out of sugar and cream together with white flour. They have an appearance of glutinous rice, and after being baked in an asbestos stove, are cut into square pieces. Their rich sweetness is worth eating. Mimosa cakes are the same as *sa-ch'i-ma*, only their top is covered with red sugar giving them a pretty appearance like that of mimosa flowers.

For *ping-t'ang-hu-lu* 冰糖壺盧 one uses strips of bamboo on which are strung such things as grapes, tubers of the *shan-yao-tou* 山藥豆 (*dioscerea bulbifera*, a plant with egg-shaped tubers used for medicine), cherry-apples, and red crab-apples. These are baked with sugar until sweet and stiff, and then cooled, and when one eats them on a winter's night, they can disperse the effects of coal and charcoal fumes.[1] The *wen-p'o*(溫朴, a kind of small quince) is like a cherry in form, but hard and firm, and should be soaked in honey so as to be both sour and at the same time sweet. They are especially good for making wine go down properly. These are all Peking foods of the season[2] . . . . .

---

[1] One of the most characteristic sights at Peking New Year fairs is that of children carrying long waving sticks of these brightly-colored, sugar-covered fruits, which are decorated with little paper streamers at the end, and which occasionally fall to the ground before finally entering the mouths of their owners. It is amusing to note that the author attributes to these candied fruits the power to dissipate headaches caused by the gas from the braziers by which houses are kept warm in winter in North China.

[2] Our author follows with quotations from other books which describe how various sweetmeats, for the most part bearing Mongol names and unknown to-day, were formerly presented to officials on such days as the winter equinox and the eighth day of the fourth month.

MANCHU CAKES

Shui-wu-t'a 水 烏 他 cakes are made from kumiss together with sugar, and are cooked during the night when the weather has become extremely cold. Their pure whiteness is like frost, and when one has them in one's mouth, it is as if one were crunching on snow. They have thus a special flavor of the north. They are made into the shapes of plum flowers, or that of squares joined at the corners, and are put in small boxes. *Nai-wu-t'a* 奶 烏 他 are practically the same, but their taste is somewhat inferior.

Note : These are Manchu delicacies, as shown both by their names and by the use of kumiss, a typical nomad food. They are hardly known to-day.

FRUITS OF THE SEASON

Each year during the tenth month are to be found in the shops such fruits as the *ch'ih pao-er* 赤 包 兒 (*thladiantha dubia*) and *tou-ku-niang* 鬥 姑 娘 (*solanum sp.*) The former is produced on a vine and has the shape of a sweet melon, but smaller. By the early part of winter it is red and soft, and may be played with (but cannot be eaten). The latter has a shape of a small egg-plant, and is as red as coral, round, glossy, and slippery. Children all like it, and therefore it is called *tou-ku-niang* (literally " fighting girls," that is, fighting for its possession). The Japanese quince is two inches in size, and is green rather than yellow. Its fragrance, in comparison with the quinces from the south, is even more penetrating. The *wen-p'o* 溫 朴 (*cydonia oblonga*) has a form like an orange or a pumelo, is hard and firm, and is like the quince in its characteristics, but has hair. If one uses it to perfume clothing, its fragrance will last a month without disappearing. These too are all products of the season.

BIRDS OF THE SEASON

The coming of the birds has a very close connection with the seasons, and in Peking from the tenth month onward, there are such birds as the hawfinch. The hawfinch is six or seven inches in length, with an ash-colored body, black wings, yellow bill, and short tail. Boys of the city buy and train it until it can catch small pellets tossed in the air. . . . . .

The crossbill is four or five inches long, with the parts of its bill crossing each other from the left and right, thus distinguishing the female and male.[1] It is red and yellow, and those which are tamed and trained can open a lock (i.e., pull the top off a small box), and take out a flag from it in their bills.

The mealy redpoll (a kind of finch) is smaller than a sparrow, and the top of its head is red. Its tricks are like those of the crossbill, but its cleverness surpasses it.

The Japanese hawfinch has a form like the hawfinch, but with a black bill. Its tricks are the same while its price is cheaper, so that there are some gourmands who like to eat it.

The mountain finch is like a swallow in appearance. It too can catch pellets in the air, while it flies especially quickly.

These birds are all in Peking at this time. As to the wild geese of the autumn, and the swallows which arrive upon the days of worship to the soil (she jih 社 日),[2] they are always here with the regularity of the calendar.

BAMBOO SHOOTS AND 'SILVER' FISH

During the tenth month when bamboo shoots and "silver" fish (yin yü 銀 魚, i.e., salanx hyalocranius, a kind of salmon) first arrive at the Capital, they are taken from Ch'ung Wen Men by the Supervisor there, and presented to the Emperor, according to custom, in the same way as is the yellow trout of the third month.[3]

---

[1] One of which supposedly has its beak crossed in one direction, the other in the other.

[2] The name given to two days, one in spring, the other in autumn, when offerings were anciently made to the God of the Soil. They occur, respectively, on the fifth wu 戊 day after the Beginning of Spring, and Beginning of Autumn, that is, fairly close to the spring and autumn equinoxes.

[3] Cf. p. 35.

CHAPTER XI—THE ELEVENTH MONTH

JACKETS TURNED INSIDE OUT (*Fan Kua Tzǔ* 翻 掛 子)

ON the first day of the eleventh month those officials who have the right from the Emperor to wear sable furs, all put them on as one man, and these are called " jackets turned inside out."

Note: So named because the fur on them faces outward, instead of lining the inner side, as is the more usual Chinese custom.

MOON DIRECTLY OVERHEAD (*Yüeh Tang T'ou* 月 當 頭)

On the fifteenth day of the eleventh month, the moon is directly overhead.[1] If one meets it at its time of fullness, the shadow of a tower will be without any point, and a man's shadow will also look extremely short. Small boys and girls who like to have fun ought not to sleep on this night so that after waiting until the moon is directly overhead and is looking down, they may select some shadow to look at.

WINTER SOLSTICE (*Tung Chih* 冬 至)

The winter solstice is a festival for the sacrifice to Heaven, and a time at which the various officials present their felicitations.[2] Among the people it is not a festival, and they simply eat *hun-tun* (餛 飩, a kind of pork dumpling), just as they eat noodles at the summer solstice. Therefore a Peking proverb says : " *Hun-tun* at the winter solstice ; at the summer solstice, noodles." [3]

According to the *Han Shu*, at the winter solstice the *yang* fluid rises, and the way of the ruler correspondingly lengthens, so that he is thereby congratulated. At the summer solstice the *yin* fluid rises, and therefore no congratulations are offered.[4] . . . .

[1] This is the full moon which falls closest to the winter solstice, and hence the one when the moon in its orbit is almost perpendicular in the northern latitudes.

[2] This was the sacrifice made to Heaven by the Emperor at the Altar of Heaven.

[3] *Tung chih hun-tun, hsia chih mien* 冬 至 餛 飩，夏 至 麵.

[4] That is, at the winter solstice, when the days are shortest, the female *yin* principle has reached its apogee and thereafter declines, while the male *yang* correspondingly increases.

天壇采藥

ALTAR OF HEAVEN

'NINE NINES' CHART OF LESSENING COLD

The chart of lessening cold (*hsiao han t'u* 消寒圖) is composed of nine patterns, (each made up of a series of nine small circles arranged in rows of three, making a total of) eighty-one small circles. Starting from the winter solstice, one circle is marked off each day, a mark

---

The opposite is true at the summer solstice. This quotation, allegedly from the *Han Shu*, actually comes from the *Tu Tuan* 獨斷 by Ts'ai Yung 蔡邕 (A.D. 132-192), as cited in the commentary to the *Hou Han Shu* (History of the Later Han Dynasty), Chap. 15, section on the winter solstice. Our author follows the quotation with a somewhat forced explanation of the origin of the term *hun-tun*.

on the top indicating cloudy weather, on the bottom clear weather, on the left wind, on the right rain, and snow in the center.

Note: Thus each pattern is arranged as, for example, as follows:

1. ◒	4. ◑	7. ○
2. ◓	5. ⊙	8. ○
3. ◐	6. ○	9. ○

In this chart, circle 1 indicates clouds; 2 indicates clear weather; 3 wind; 4 rain; and 5 snow. A series of nine such patterns gives a total of eighty-one circles, on which may be kept a daily record of the weather during the eighty-one days following the winter solstice (i.e., usually from December 22 to March 12), by which time the winter cold is over.

According to the *Ti-ching Ching-wu-lüeh*, on the winter solstice families would paint a plum branch in outline, (having on it nine blossoms with a total of) eighty-one petals. Each day someone would mark a petal (in accordance with the system described above), so that by the time the petals were finished, the nine nines of days would all have appeared, and spring would then be far advanced. This was called the " nine nines " chart of lessening cold.

I myself as a boy did this sort of thing, and can it not be said, then, to have been in essential agreement with antiquity?

Note: There is another method even more sophisticated than that of the painting of the plum flower. This is to write a series of nine characters, such as those given in the following lines, which were once observed written on a wall in the Forbidden City:

庭 前 垂 柳 *T'ing ch'ien ch'ui liu*

茂 草 待 春 風 *Mao ts'ao tai ch'un feng*

Which may be translated as:
" Before the hall droop the willows;
The luxuriant herbage awaits the winds of spring."
Readers acquainted with Chinese will notice that each character is made up of nine strokes, thus making once more a total of eighty-one strokes. Like the plum flower, the characters are drawn in hollow outline only, so that they may be filled in in the same way. As the strokes of Chinese characters are always written in a definite order, there can be no mistake as to which day has been indicated.

ICE SLEIGHS

From the winter solstice onward, when stretches of water are once more frozen, such places as the Lake of Ten Temples, the city moat, and the Second Sluice (on the canal running from Peking to

T'ung Chou) all have their " ice beds ",¹ which when pulled by one man, are exceedingly rapid in movement. They are about five feet long, three feet broad, and are made of wood. They have iron runners on the bottom, and can seat three or four people. To ride in one after the snow has cleared away and when the sun is warm, is like moving within a cup of jade, and is a joyful thing indeed. But after the Beginning of Spring (i.e., about February 6) one cannot ride in them, for if one does so it is extremely dangerous. Thus there are instances of people who have fallen into holes in the ice, while the man who pulled them ran away.

At the present time princes and great officials who have obtained the kind command of the Emperor to do so, are also permitted inside the Hsi Yüan Men (the east entrance to the Central Lake or Chung Hai) to go riding on a pulled sleigh. These sleighs are most beautifully decorated, with a covering like a carriage top, able to withstand wind and snow.

According to the *I-ch'ing-ko Tsa-ch'ao*, during the Ming dynasty people who enjoyed such things were always to be found at the Pool of Heaped-up Waters (Chi Shui T'an), who for the sport of it would tie ten odd sleighs together, take with them a basket of food and some wine, spread a rug over the top of the sleighs, and there drink wildly in the middle of the ice until intoxicated—truly sport only for a robust and vigorous man !

SKATING

Ice-shoes are made of steel, having a single runner in the middle which is fastened to the shoe above. As one raises one's body there comes movement which cannot be stopped. Skilful adepts, who skate like a dragon-fly brushing the water, or a swallow piercing the waves, are especially worth watching.

According to the *Jih-hsia*, when the ice froze at the T'ai I Ch'ih ² during the winter months, those who liked this exercise used to be

---

¹ *Ping ch'uang* 冰 牀, i.e., ice sleighs, also commonly known as *p'ai tzŭ* 排 子.

² A general term for the three lakes west of the Forbidden City : the Pei Hai, Chung Hai, and Nan Hai.

金鰲歸里

NORTHERN LAKE OR PEI HAI

Note the exaggerated elevation given the famous marble bridge, a convention to be found
both in Chinese and in medieval European drawings.

given rewards by the Emperor so as to maintain their martial spirit,
improve the national morals, etc.

CUTTING OF ICE

During the three nine-day periods following the winter solstice,
the ice is hard and is cut up during the night (for summer use) with
a sound as of chiselling stone. This is called " striking ice " (*ta ping*
打 冰). But after these three periods of nine days, even though the
ice is still hard, it cannot be used.

According to the *Shih-wu Yüan-hui*, King Ch'eng of the Chou dynasty (1115-1079 B.C.) commanded that there be an " ice man " in charge of ice, and decreed that in the twelfth month of the year the ice should be cut and stored in ice " retreats," that is, what would to-day be called ice-houses. The twelfth month of the Chou dynasty corresponded to the tenth month of the present calendar, and thus we can see how the regulations for the storage of ice had already begun at this early date.

> *Note*: In the *Shih Ching* (Book of Odes), I, Bk. XV, Ode i, Stanza 8, one of the earliest Chinese literary works, there is an interesting reference to the cutting and storing of ice, and sacrifice to the spirit of the ice :
>
> > " In the days of the second month, they hew out the ice with harmonious blows ;
> > And in those of the third month, they convey it to the ice-houses,
> > (Which they open) in those of the fourth, early in the morning,
> > A lamb having been offered in sacrifice with scallions."
>
> Though the months as given here do not tally with those mentioned above, they would seem to be more in accord with what would be the coldest time of year.

DISTRIBUTION OF SABLES

Each year at the coming of the winter months the members of the Imperial Bodyguard stationed at the Ch'ien Ch'ing Men and at the big gates (of the Forbidden City), etc., are each given money by their officers for sable jackets, each man thus receiving several tens of taels.[1]

---

[1] This sum would be quite inadequate to buy such an expensive fur as sable, and the term " sable " is probably a euphemism here for some other cheaper variety of fur.

CHAPTER XII—THE TWELFTH MONTH

EIGHTH DAY OF THE TWELFTH MONTH GRUEL (*La Pa Chou* 臘 八 粥)

Note: The word *la* is the name of a sacrifice going back into early Chinese history. The sacrifice took place each year shortly after the winter solstice and was made by the ruler to his ancestors and to the five tutelary spirits of the house: those of the door, main gate, kitchen stove, center of house or impluvium, and well or, according to some, alley. It was a sacrifice of thanksgiving for bounteous harvests. *Cf.* the *Li Chi*, in *Sacred Books of the East*, XXVII, 300. Because of this ceremony, the entire twelfth month has come to be known as the *la* month, so that *la pa* gruel really means gruel of the eighth day of the twelfth month. The term also has been taken over by Buddhism as the name for an offering made to Buddha on this day.

For *la pa* gruel one uses glutinous millet, white rice, glutinous rice, canary seed, water-chestnuts, chestnuts, small red beans, and dates from which the skin has been removed, boiled with water. On the exterior, so as to give spots of color, are used peach seeds for their red color, almonds, melon seeds, peanuts, hazelnuts, and pine seeds, as well as white and red sugar and raisins. It is imperative not to use lotus seeds, flat beans, seeds of the *i* 薏 (*coix lachryma*, a kind of small water-lily), or *kuei yüan* 桂 元 (dried *nephelium longana*, a southern fruit similar to, but smaller than the lichee), which if utilized will spoil the taste.

Every year on the seventh day of the twelfth month, fruits are peeled and utensils washed, and this work is continued the whole night until at break of day the gruel is cooked. Besides offering it in sacrifice to one's ancestors and to Buddha, one makes presents of it to one's relatives and friends, but this should not be done after midday. At the same time one makes figures of lions out of red dates, peach seeds, etc. to be put on top of the gruel, whereby children may give expression to their ingenuity.

According to the *Yen-tu Yu-lan-chih*, the Emperor on the eighth day of the twelfth month would present gruel to the various officials, while the common people also made *la pa* gruel out of various grains and fruits, that with the most varieties being the best.

Though to-day there is no such presentation to the various officials, rich families still make presents of it, competing with each other in clever attempts at originality. Comparing them with the people of former times, there are some to-day who surpass them, but none who do not equal them.

PICKLED OR 'BIG' CABBAGE

"Big cabbage" is cabbage which has been pickled, and every household which makes a present of *la pa* gruel must complete the gift with this. According to the vegetable's good or bad quality, one can predict the future prosperity or decline of the house (of its maker).

According to the *Kuang-ch'ün-fang-p'u*, one name for cabbage was *sung* 菘. In the north it used to be commonly put in a cellar where it would see neither air nor sun, and in which it would put forth shoots which were all delicate and yellow in color, of incomparable tenderness. These were called yellow shoots, and were considered to constitute a separate sort of cabbage.

But people who eat such things to-day simply separate the outer skin of the cabbage from its heart, (which they eat as a substitute for these shoots), and which hence cannot be considered as a distinct variety.

BOILED GRUEL AT THE 'LAMA TEMPLE' (*Yung Ho Kung*)

The priests of the Yung Ho Kung boil gruel on the night of the eighth day, which they offer to Buddha, at which time the Emperor specially delegates some important official to witness the ceremony, so as to manifest his sincere respect. The size of the kettle used for this gruel is sufficient to contain several *tan*.[1]

IMPERIAL DISTRIBUTION OF DEER

Every year in the twelfth month there is a presentation to the princes and great officials of spotted deer and ordinary deer (which have been sent as tribute to Court from Mongolia, etc.). The arrival of the time is announced by the Imperial Household Department, whereupon each yamen must send someone to receive its share. But officials from the third grade down do not receive anything.

---

[1] A *tan* 石 is equivalent in capacity to 1.03 hectolitres.

Putting Away the Seals (*Feng Yin* 封 印)

Every year in the twelfth month, some time during the four-day period of the nineteenth, twentieth, twenty-first, and twenty-second days, the Imperial Board of Astronomy selects a propitious time on which, according to rule, it announces that seals are to be put away,[1] and this is promulgated to the entire country, which acts upon it like a single body. On the day of putting away the seals, the Keeper of the Seals of each Ministry and Department must invite his co-workers to form a jolly group and drink gaily together, pledging each other in wine over the year's labors. Thus each time when the seals have been put away, it is as if ten thousand riders had appeared at once, so that the Ch'ien Men district is extraordinarily crowded, and restaurants and amusement places are all equally full. After this putting away of the seals, beggars who lack means of support may snatch goods from shops without the least hesitation, showing how bad a custom it is for the officials not to be going about their business.[2]

Closing of the Theatres

After the putting away of the seals, theatres select a day on which to close. The eight theatrical companies of the City unite to give a performance (the proceeds from which are given to the theatre employees, after which there are no more plays) until the arrival of New Year's Day, when the play, " Conferring Happiness " (*Tz'ŭ Fu* 賜 福) opens the theatrical season. This in truth serves to bring in with song a year of tranquillity.

Looking at the plays presented in Peking, one can see that the taste of different times has varied. Thus before and during the period of Hsien Feng (1851-1861), the *k'un* 崑 [3] and *kao* 高 or *i* 弋 types of drama were most valued. The *kao* form has gongs and drums, but is without stringed and bamboo instruments, and its sad songs

---

[1] I.e., all official work ceases until the opening of the seals again after New Year, about one month later, for which *cf*. p. 9.

[2] That is, the New Year holidays allow beggars and thieves to become bolder since the officials who would ordinarily deal with them are on vacation.

[3] A slow and plaintive type of music which originated during the Ming dynasty, and is related to the following type.

are in the old taste of the Capital. From the time of Hsien Feng onward the " two flute " (*er huang* 二 簧) form has been especially favored.[1] In recent times the *ch'in* 秦 form has been equally valued, and is the same as what is commonly called the *pang-tzŭ* type.[2]

There are no theatres in the Inner (i.e., Tartar) City, these being all in the Outer (or Chinese) City. This is probably because of the fear that the soldiers of the Eight Banners (stationed in the Tartar City) might become accustomed to idle pleasures.

Besides the legitimate stage, there are such forms of entertainment as puppet-shows, shadow-plays, tambourines, *shih-pu-hsien* 什 不 閑, *tzŭ-ti-shu* 子 弟 書, variety vaudeville, *pa-shih* 把 式, sound imitators, "big drums," and story-tellers. . . . . In the shadow-plays, a light

SHADOW-PLAY FIGURES

is used to produce a shadow.[3] They give extraordinary impressions of sorrow and anger, and when old women listen to them many of them are compelled to drop tears. The tambourine form is made up of a few people of the lower class, some of whom play stringed instruments, while others sing; the buffoonery which they strike up makes one laugh very much. The *shih-pu-hsien* has a *tan* (旦, a man who plays a feminine character) and a comedian (*ch'ou* 丑), but no leading character (*sheng* 生). They sing a special type of song, the while sinking and rising and winsomely circling, delightfully coming and going incessantly. In the time of Hsien Feng (1851-1861) and T'ung

---

[1] So called because in this type two flutes were originally used. Now, however, they are used only in the wedding and funeral scenes, etc.

[2] The *pang-tzŭ* 梆 子 consists of two pieces of wood, one struck against the other. This form originated in Shensi and Shansi, supposedly during the reign of Ming Huang (713-755), and is called the *ch'in* type because the State of Ch'in, which first unified China in 221 B.C., occupied the territory now comprising these provinces.

[3] The jointed figures are cut out of semi-transparent sheets of donkey skin, beautifully colored so that colored shadows are thrown upon a screen stretched in front.

Chih (1862-1874) and before, they were especially esteemed, but in recent times they have disappeared like Kuang Ling.[1]

The songs of the *tzŭ-ti-shu* are sad and lovely, and their words are refined. Variety vaudeville and the *pa-shih* consist, respectively, of miscellaneous entertainments and of military arts (such as sword dancing). Sound imitators use their mouths to imitate the sound of various birds, reproduce northern and southern accents, and simulate joy, laughter, sorrow, and reviling, all combined in one man in such a way that listeners can distinguish all these things in every detail.

The arts of the "big drum" and the story-teller can have an especially harmful effect on people's minds. This is because the "big drum" (which is singing and dancing done by female performers), concerns itself for the most part with matters relating to the "picking of valerian," and "presentation of small peonies,"[2] while the mere singing and posturing by women is in itself already something improper. The story-teller simply gesticulates and talks, without any assisting music, and by his words makes bravoes and desperadoes come into movement as if alive. When townspeople listen to such things, it is easy to instil in them ideas of creating disorder and doing evil. Hence persons who have a mind for the morals of the people should be thinking about prohibiting such as this.

RELEASE FROM STUDIES

After the putting away of seals, schoolboys are released from the establishments of their private tutors, this being called "release from the year's studies."

---

[1] 廣 陵 an old name for Yang Chou, once a city of great importance on the Grand Canal in Kiangsu, which had already then quite lost its preeminent position.

[2] These terms occur in the *Shih Ching*, I, Bk. VII, Ode xxi, Stanza 1, in which they refer to free love. According to Legge's translation, the stanza runs :

The Tsin and the Wei	But let us go again to see.
Now present their broad sheets of water.	Beyond the Wei,
Ladies and gentlemen	The ground is large and fit for pleasure."
Are carrying flowers of valerian.	So the gentlemen and ladies,
A lady says, " Have you been to see ?"	Made sport together,
A gentleman replies, " I have been.	Presenting one another with small peonies.

Sacrifice to the 'God of the Kitchen' (*Tsao Chün* 竈 君)

On the twenty-third day sacrifices are made to the God of the Kitchen. In olden times an antelope was used, and in recent times I have heard of them still being used within the Palace. But I have not seen them used among the people. When the common people sacrifice to the Kitchen God, they simply use *nan-t'ang* 南 糖 and *kuan-tung* 關 東 candies and sugar cakes, together with pure water, grass, and beans. The candy is sacrificed to the god, and the clear water, grass, and beans to the god's horse.

> *Note* : On this day the Kitchen God is supposed to ascend to Heaven to report on the family's behaviour throughout the year. Therefore sweet foods are given him, so that, as some say, he will report only sweet things ; or, according to others, so that his mouth will be so sticky that he cannot speak.

After the sacrifice is finished, the picture of the god is taken down and burned together with *ch'ien chang* and *yüan pao* (paper spirit-money). But on New Year's Eve, at the time of meeting the spirits, a new picture of him is put up. On this day (i.e., the twenty-third) there are many fire-crackers, and the day is commonly called the "little New Year" (*hsiao nien* 小 年).

According to the *Jih-hsia*, in Peking it is only men who, in accord with old custom, would worship the Kitchen God, while women were forbidden to preside at the sacrifice.[1] The time of worship fell on the twenty-third day, but people coming from the south would do it on the twenty-fourth. This account is in accord with what Liu T'ung (one of the authors of the *Ti-ching Ching-wu-lüeh*) also says.

'Spring Couplets' (*Ch'un Lien* 春 聯)

"Spring couplets" are the same as peach charms (*t'ao fu* 桃 符).[2] From the twelfth month onward, there are professional scribes who sit in front of shops writing these "spring couplets" and hoping to earn money by their fine calligraphy. After the sacrifice to the Kitchen

---

[1] *Cf.* p. 64.

[2] These were boards made of peach wood, painted with pictures of gate gods or with charm inscriptions, and put on the sides of doors. The peach, the Taoist symbol of immortality, is supposed to have magical powers (see the Hall of Spiral Peaches on p. 28). In later times these have been replaced by " spring couplets " such as here described.

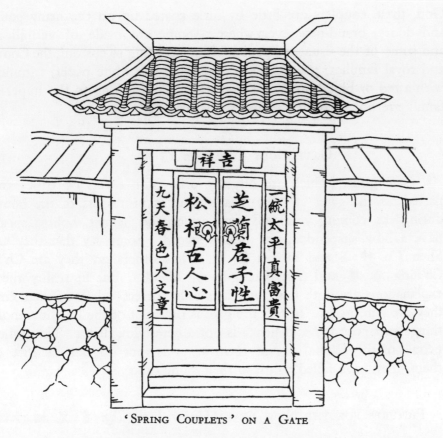

'Spring Couplets' on a Gate

Above the door panels in the illustration given above appear the two characters, *chi hsiang* 吉祥, meaning "fortunate and auspicious." The two lines on either side of the door panels read:

I t'ung t'ai p'ing chen fu kuei, 一統太平真富貴,
Chiu t'ien ch'un se ta wen chang. 九天春色大文章.

"May there be a single universal peace, with true wealth and honor.
May the spring colors of the Nine Heavens appear in profuse elegance."

Ch'ü Yüan, in his poem *T'ien Wen* (Questions about Heaven), conceives of the Nine Heavens as rising one above another in nine storeys. The *Huai Nan Tzŭ* (compiled under the Prince of Huai Nan who died in 122 B.C., Chap. 3) describes them as the eight heavens of the eight compass points, surrounding a single central heaven. Nine is the Chinese lucky number (*cf.* p. 65, and note 1 on p. 69), and this symmetrical laying out of the celestial regions is an interesting example of the Chinese attempt ever to give harmony and balance to their conceptions of cosmology.

On the two door panels themselves appear the lines:

Chih lan chün tzŭ hsing, 芝蘭君子性, "The epidendrum is the nature of the Superior Man.
Sung po ku jen hsin. 松柏古人心. The pine and cypress are the heart of the men of old."

The epidendrum (*chih lan* 芝蘭) is symbolic of purity and steadfastness, this idea originating

God, these couplets are little by little pasted up on the many gates and doors, brand-new everywhere. Some are made of vermilion, and some of the usual red paper. But according to custom, the Court and royal families, princes and dukes, etc., use white paper, trimmed with a red or blue border. Those who do not belong to the Imperial family are not permitted to use such varieties.

GATE GODS (*Men Shen* 門 神)

Gate gods, (which are brightly printed on sheets of paper and pasted on the gates at New Year's time as protectors of the house during the coming year), all wear armor and helmet, hold a spear, have a bow suspended, and bear a sword. Some say that they are Shen T'u 神 荼 and Yü Lei 鬱 壘,[1] while others say they are Ch'in Ch'iung 秦 瓊 and (Hu) Ching-te 胡 敬 德.[2] But in reality these explanations are both false, and it is only correct to say of them that they are gate gods. In fact the gate is the chief of the five household things sacrificed to,[3] and hence is not a heterodox deity. Thus when people of the Capital regard them as gods, but do not sacrifice to them, they have failed to grasp their significance.

PICTURES FOR THE NEW YEAR (*Hua-er P'eng Tzǔ* 畫 兒 棚 子)

Each year during the twelfth month mat-sheds are put up in busy parts of the city for the sale of prints. Women and children compete

---

in a passage (section 20) of the *K'ung Tzǔ Chia Yü* (Sayings of the Confucian School), in which it is said : " The epidendrum, growing in the deep forest, lacks not fragrance merely because no man is there ; the Superior Man, practising morality and virtue, does not allow his purity to become deteriorated by any difficulties." Likewise the pine and cypress, because they are always green and are long-lived, symbolize the men of old. Thus in the *Shih Ching*, II, Decade I, Ode VI, Stanza 6, the noble guests who have been feasted by the king express their thanks in song, and sing that he may be : " Never waning, never falling, Like the luxuriance of the pine and cypress."

[1] Two brothers with supernatural powers, who are said once to have summoned all the spirits before them, seized those who had been injurious to mankind, bound them with reed withes, and given them as food to tigers.

[2] These two heroes were faithful followers of T'ang T'ai Tsung (627-649), and guarded him from all harm. Hence in commemoration of them the Emperor had their pictures painted on his palace doors, and from these, according to this theory, the gate gods originated.

[3] For these, *cf.* p. 4.

By courtesy of Miss Mabel E. Tom

IN AN OLD MANCHU HOUSEHOLD

shaved for the occasion by one of
y seen in Peking. To the right all
red. Boxes containing the artificial
ɲ in their hair are seen carried in by
ɑn is pasting a gate god. On the
ɪng, sits the old grandmother, prob-

ably the ruler of the house, to whom New Year presents are
being offered. Still to her right stands a man holding strings of
cash. In the foreground another is painting " spring couplets "
(*ch'un lien*) to be pasted on the doors. The original of this picture
is almost five times the size of the reproduction.

The bow and arrows hanging on the left wall shows this to be in all probability a Manchu family, for the Manchus long kept up their nomadic tradition. The table below is loaded with firecrackers for the New Year, and beneath it the protruding ends of Chinese cabbage appear. The maidservant going out by the left door is carrying *man-t'ou*, or Chinese bread. In the left foreground

a small child is having its head
the itinerant barbers common
sorts of foods are being prep
flowers worn by Chinese wom
the main door, on which a
extreme right, on the heated *k*

with each other in buying them, for these too serve to mark the yearly festivities.[1]

NEW YEAR'S EVE (*Ch'u Hsi* 除夕)

Pekinese call the evening of the thirtieth day the *Ch'u Hsi*. On the clear morning of this day the Emperor receives congratulations in his audience hall,[2] and minor servitors pay visits to their superior officials, which is called paying one's respects for the year to one's officials. Houses having hereditary titles sacrifice at their ancestral shrines and hang up the ancestral pictures.

After twilight, the entire household sits together to pass out the year. Wine and refreshments are laid out; the lamps and candles give forth their calm light; and women and children all amuse themselves by throwing dice or playing cards. During the *hai* (nine to eleven p.m.) and *tzŭ* (eleven p.m. to one a.m.) periods, when the sky has become even more black, and the fire-crackers outside have become still noisier, incense is burned on a table which has been arranged, to meet the spirits who descend to earth at this time. (After this, the entire family) sleeps together with their clothes on for a little time until the coming of morning, when the bright sun shows in the window, and the sound of fire-crackers greets the ears. Thereupon the people of the household offer congratulations to one another, and a joyful atmosphere fills the room. Within the twinkling of an eye, lo! another year has been met!

YEARLY BRANCH TREADING (*Hsi Sui* 躧歲)

On New Year's Eve all places that may be walked on, extending from the doors of the rooms to the main gate, are covered with scattered sesamum stalks. . . . .

Note: These by their crackling might serve to give warning of the approach of any spirits on this evening.

---

[1] These picture sheets, printed very cheaply in large quantities, represent scenes of New Year rejoicing, of the God of Wealth, scenes from the stage, etc.

[2] These are congratulations offered only by members of the royal family and closely connected officials. The general audience for all officials comes on New Year's Day. *Cf.* p. 1.

New Year's Pudding (*Nien Fan* 年 飯)

Nien fan is made out of millet and rice, on top of which are set pine and cypress branches, to which metal coins, dates, chestnuts, *lung yen* 龍 眼 (the *nephelium longana*), and sticks of incense are tied. After the *P'o Wu*,[1] this is disposed of.

Hall Flowers (*T'ang Hua* 唐 花)

Flowers which have been reared by artificial heat are always called *t'ang* flowers by florists, and at every New Year people make presents of them to one another. Thus peonies everywhere stand now in lovely disarray, and kumquat plants droop their yellow fruit confusedly, their warm fragrance filling the nostrils. The delicate beauty of the three spring months is all here within one hall, which is why they are called " hall flowers."

According to the *Jih-hsia*, peonies, plum and red-peach blossoms, and jasmine are sold in Peking during the twelfth month, having all been reared in hot-houses by means of fire. . . . . This method has been in existence since the Han dynasty, when in the gardens of great officials, shallot, onion, and madder used to be covered over in long sheds, and kept warm by fire day and night, so that these various vegetables, receiving the warm air, would all sprout. But Shao Hsin-ch'en, who was Minister of Natural Resource Revenues (in 33 B.C.), said that these were all untimely things, which would be injurious to men and inauspicious as offerings, and so asked that they be done away with.

Again, a T'ang dynasty poem says :

> " The warm water is distributed inside the garden,
> And in the middle decade (eleventh to twentieth) of the second month, the melons are already advanced." [2]

This also has reference to this practice.

---

[1] The fifth day of the first month. *Cf.* p. 3.

[2] *Nei yüan fen te wen t'ang shui*, 內 園 分 得 溫 湯 水,

Erh yüeh chung hsün i chin kua. 二 月 中 旬 巳 進 瓜.

TIBETAN INCENSE

The so-called Tibetan incense is made in Tibet, and has a rich thick flavor. It is composed of garoo wood, sandalwood, and sapan wood. At the end of each year it is burned in the homes of noble families throughout the night so that its fragrance fills the nostrils, reaching even to the points of the eaves and corners of the rooms. Truly is it an aristocrat among incenses.

MONEY TREE (*Yao Ch'ien Shu* 搖 錢 樹)

For this one takes large pine and cypress branches, sticks them into a vase, and ties old coins, *yüan pao*, and paper pomegranate flowers, etc., on them, this being called the " tree from which one shakes money."

> *Note:* It is curious to find here a custom reminiscent of our own decorated Christmas trees. This money tree, of course, is expected to bring material prosperity to the home during the coming year.

CASH TO PASS THE YEAR (*Ya Sui Ch'ien* 歷 歲 錢)

With colored string one threads together some copper cash so arranged as to make the form of a dragon. This is put at the foot of the bed (of children), and is called " cash to pass the year "; and when it is given by old people to children it is also called by this name.

> *Note:* The dragon is a creature of good omen, and will protect the children during the coming year. This money is not intended to be spent, but is to be saved in order to take the child from the old year to the new, and to be held as a reserve for the year to come.

RED MONEY-NOTES

The notes issued by money-shops in exchange for coins are called *p'iao tzŭ* 票 子, and at the end of the year rich and noble families change their silver for these, to make which colored fancy paper is especially used to be written on at this time. These are called " red notes," and convey the ideas of beauty and good luck.

LUCKY TALISMANS (*Kua Ch'ien* 掛 千)

To make *kua ch'ien* one uses some lucky words, cut out in red pieces of paper, these being somewhat more than a foot long.[1] These

---

[1] That is, the pieces of paper are not themselves cut out into the form of characters, but are left as squares or oblongs into which a delicate filigree pattern is cut in such a way that the characters appear in the design between the openings cut into the paper.

are pasted up on the front of the gate, being similar in appearance to the " peach charms." Those talismans in which the forms of the Eight Immortals have been cut out, are the kind hung up in front of images of divinities.[1] Such things are much used by the common people, but rarely by the great hereditary families. Those of yellow paper three inches long, and of red paper a little over an inch long, are called small *kua ch'ien*, and are used by shops.

TABLE OF HEAVEN AND EARTH (*T'ien Ti Cho* 天 地 桌)

Every New Year's Eve a long table is set out in the courtyard, on which the " hundred divisions" (*po-fen* 百 分) is offered. The *po-fen* (is a large sheet of yellow paper on which) is a complete re-presentation of all the heavenly deities and sages.   In front of this is laid a row of " honey offerings " (*mi kung* 蜜 供),[2] and then apples, dried fruits, breads, vegetables, and New Year cakes (*nien kao* 年 糕), each in one row.   This is called the " complete offering."   Above the offering hang figures of the Eight Immortals, threaded together by *t'ung ts'ao* (*akebia quinata*, a climbing plant used in medicine), together with paper pomegranate flowers, *yüan pao*, etc., which are all called "flowers offered to the gods."   At the time of the " meeting of the spirits,"[3] the *po-fen* is burned, but the offering is perpetuated after this by incense burning, which continues until the Lantern Festival.   This whole affair is called the " Table of Heaven and Earth."[4]

MI KUNG CANDY OFFERINGS

---

[1] These Eight Immortals were eight men who, for various reasons, became Taoist Immortals. Three were historical persons, while the rest are figures of romance.   The legend concerning them as a group probably does not antedate the Sung dynasty (906-1280), though many of them were earlier celebrated individually as Immortals in Taoist writings.   They form one of the most popular subjects of artistic representation.

[2] Oblong sticks of yellow candy, often seen on altars as offerings, piled up like blocks into the form of a small pyramid.

[3] *Cf.* p. 101.

[4] That is, it is an offering to all the spirits in Heaven and Earth.   For a complete list of the hundred divinities represented, *cf.* Grube, *Zur Pekinger Volkskunde*, pp. 53-62.

LUCKY TALISMAN OR *Kua Ch'ien*

The four characters in the middle are 大 發 財 源 *ta fa ts'ai yüan*, which may be translated as, "May there be a great outpouring of the source of wealth." The original *kua ch'ien*, which is cut out of red paper, is one foot four inches tall, and one foot wide.

LI OF THE IRON CRUTCH

Li T'ieh Kuai, one of the Eight Taoist
Immortals.

FAREWELL TO THE OLD YEAR (*Tz'ŭ Sui* 辭 歲)

Every New Year's Eve one makes visits in one's ceremonial robes
to relatives and friends, this being called " bidding farewell to the old
year." And when the people of the house pay their respects to the
family elders, it is also called by this term. Likewise men who have
been newly married must go to the house of their wife's parents
to bid farewell to the old year, for if they do not, it is considered
discourteous.

WELCOME TO THE ' GOD OF JOY ' (*Hsi Shen* 喜 神)

On New Year's Eve the time from the " meeting of the spirits "
onward is considered as the New Year. On the occasion when one
first leaves the house at this time, one should bid welcome to the God
of Joy and bow to him.

> *Note:* Curiously enough, this god is identified with Chou Hsin 紂 辛 (1154?-1123? B.C.),
> the cruel and infamous last ruler of the Shang dynasty, who, according to the legends,
> formed a " lake of wine " at his palace, caused the trees to be hung with viands, and
> set men and women, naked, to chase each other before his eyes. It is perhaps because
> of his love of debauchery and licentiousness that he has become one of the gods of
> marriage.

POSTSCRIPT

Descriptions of sight-seeing places would seem to be out of place
in a work which records annual events. Yet these places for the
most part have fixed seasons when they are visited, and hence are
appropriate in such an annual record. Places lacking such fixed
visiting times have not been recorded here, so as to maintain this
distinction.

Written by Tun-ch'ung on the sixteenth day of the third month
of the twenty-sixth year of Kuang Hsü, that is, the cyclical year *Keng-
tzŭ* (April 15, 1900).

Additional Postscript : This record has everywhere followed
accurate historical material. The things described in it are most
varied and miscellaneous, so that it will be difficult not to criticize it
for being confused and mixed-up. Yet its purpose, after all, has been
to include nothing outside the four classes of customs, sight-seeing
places, natural products, and amusements ; which has also been the
general plan of the (*Jih-hsia*) *Chiu-wen-k'ao.*

THE CHINESE CALENDAR

As is well known, the Chinese old style calendar is a lunar rather than a solar one, being made up of twelve lunar months of twenty-nine or thirty days each, to which, because these months fail to make the required total of $365\frac{1}{4}$ days in a solar year, an intercalary month (*jun yüeh* 閏 月) is added every two or three years to make good the annual deficiency. This intercalary month must be inserted seven times every nineteen years, in such a way that the winter solstice will always fall in the eleventh month, the summer solstice in the fifth, the spring equinox in the second, and the autumn equinox in the eighth. It does not come as an extra month at the end of the year, but is simply inserted between two other months, so that during a year when it occurs there may be two successive fifth, sixth, or other two months, as the case may be, following one another. The first and twelfth months cannot be reduplicated in this way, however, nor can the intercalary month occur in a period during which the sun does not pass from one sign of the zodiac to another.

The Chinese New Year has not always been made to begin at the time of year that it does to-day. Thus the first month of the Chou dynasty (1122 ?-255 B.C.) began at the time that the eleventh month begins to-day, while other calendars were employed by other feudal states of the time, so that the chronology of that period is very confusing. The determination of the calendar has always been jealously guarded as a royal prerogative, and sometimes has had important political implications.[1] Since the reform of the calendar in 104 B.C., however, it has remained unchanged, with but a few brief exceptions, until the Chinese Republic discarded it in favor of the Gregorian calendar in 1912. According to this reform of 104 B.C., New Year's Day has been so arranged as to fall always on the day of the first new moon after the sun enters Aquarius, which means that it cannot come earlier than our January 21 or later than February 20.[2]

---

[1] *Cf.* Chen Chin Sien, *The Anomalous Calendars of the Ch'in and Han Dynasties and their Social and Political Significance*, in *Chinese Social and Political Science Review*, Vol. XVIII, No. 2, pp. 157-176.

[2] *Cf.* also Appendix F, giving a lunar and western concordance for 1957 to 1984.

The Chinese calendar is not exclusively a lunar one, however, for it also embraces a series of twenty-four " sections " or " joints " (*chieh* 節), which occur every fifteen days throughout the year, and are based on a solar reckoning. They are of particular value to the peasants, who follow them implicitly as a guide to indicate the proper times for sowing, harvesting, etc., and run as follows[†]:

Name	Western Calendar about	Chinese Calendar about
*1. Beginning of Spring (*Li Ch'un* 立春)	Feb. 6	26th of 12th month
2. Rain Water (*Yü Shui* 雨水)	„ 20	1st of 1st „
3. Waking of Insects (*Ching Che* 驚蟄)	Mar. 5	16th of 1st „
*4. Spring Equinox (*Ch'un Fen* 春分) ...	„ 20	1st of 2nd „
*5. Pure Brightness (*Ch'ing Ming* 清明)	April 5	16th of 2nd „
6. Corn Rain (*Ku Yü* 穀雨)	„ 20	1st of 3rd „
7. Beginning of Summer (*Li Hsia* 立夏)	May 5	17th of 3rd „
8. Grain Full (*Hsiao Man* 小滿) ...	„ 21	3rd of 4th „
9. Grain in the Ear (*Mang Chung* 芒種)	June 6	19th of 4th „
*10. Summer Solstice (*Hsia Chih* 夏至) ...	„ 21	5th of 5th „
11. Slight Heat (*Hsiao Shu* 小暑) ...	July 7	20th of 5th „
12. Great Heat (*Ta Shu* 大暑)	„ 23	6th of 6th „
13. Beginning of Autumn (*Li Ch'iu* 立秋)	Aug. 7	20th of 6th „
14. Stopping of Heat (*Ch'u Shu* 處暑) ...	„ ˙ 23	8th of 7th „
15. White Dew (*Pai Lu* 白露)	Sept. 8	24th of 7th „
*16. Autumn Equinox (*Ch'iu Fen* 秋分) ...	„ 23	9th of 8th „
17. Cold Dew (*Han Lu* 寒露)	Oct. 8	25th of 8th „
18. Frost's Descent (*Shuang Chiang* 霜降)	„ 23	11th of 9th „
19. Beginning of Winter (*Li Tung* 立冬)	Nov. 7	26th of 9th „
20. Slight Snow (*Hsiao Hsüeh* 小雪) ...	„ 22	11th of 10th „
21. Great Snow (*Ta Hsüeh* 大雪) ...	Dec. 7	25th of 10th „
*22. Winter Solstice (*Tung Chih* 冬至) ...	„ 22	11th of 11th „
23. Slight Cold (*Hsiao Han* 小寒) ...	Jan. 6	26th of 11th „
24. Great Cold (*Ta Han* 大寒)	„ 22	12th of 12th „

* Days having special observances which are described in this book.
[†]See Introduction to the Second Edition, page xix.

Chinese chronology is usually dated by means of the number of years of each Emperor's reign, or, to-day, by the year of the Republic. Thus the present year, 1935, is the twenty-fourth year of the Republic. Beginning in 163 B.C., the system of " reign titles " or *nien hao* 年 號, designations which had an auspicious meaning or which were intended to commemorate some event of their time, was instituted as titles given to successive time periods. At first these were frequently changed at the whim of the Emperor every few years within a reign. But from the Ming dynasty onward, the practice has been adopted of allowing one reign title to stand unchanged throughout the reign, with the result that the Emperors of the Ming and Ch'ing (Manchu) dynasties have come to be better known under their reign titles than under their actual dynastic titles or *miao hao* 廟 號. Thus the title, Ch'ien Lung, is really nothing more than the reign title of Emperor Kao Tsung of the Manchu dynasty, and strictly speaking refers to the period of his reign, rather than to the Emperor himself.

Still another Chinese method of chronology is that of the Ten Heavenly Stems (*T'ien Kan* 天 干) and Twelve Earthly Branches (*Ti Chih* 地 支), which appear as follows :

Ten Heavenly Stems	*Twelve Earthly Branches*
1. *Chia* 甲.	1. *Tzŭ* 子.
2. *Yi* 乙	2. *Ch'ou* 丑.
3. *Ping* 丙.	3. *Yin* 寅.
4. *Ting* 丁.	4. *Mao* 卯.
5. *Wu* 戊.	5. *Ch'en* 辰.
6. *Chi* 己.	6. *Ssŭ* 巳.
7. *Keng* 庚.	7. *Wu* 午.
8. *Hsin* 辛.	8. *Wei* 未.
9. *Jen* 壬.	9. *Shen* 申.
10. *Kuei* 癸.	10. *Yu* 酉.
	11. *Hsü* 戌.
	12. *Hai* 亥.

By combining these cyclical signs into pairs, beginning with *Chia-tzŭ* (signs 1 and 1 of each series), *Yi-ch'ou* (2 and 2), *Ping-yin* (3 and 3), etc.; going on until we reach *Chia-hsü* (1 and 11), *Yi-hai* (2 and 12), and *Ping-tzŭ* (3 and 1 again); and so continuing until each of the Stems has been combined with each of the Branches, we obtain a total series of sixty different combinations before *Chia-tzŭ*, the first pair, reappears. This gives us the famous Chinese cycle of sixty of which Tennyson wrote, at once with the ignorance and contempt of his day :

" Better fifty years of Europe than a cycle of Cathay."

But it was only beginning with the Han dynasty (206 B.C.-A.D. 220) that years were dated in cycles of sixty in this way. The Stems and Branches were used long before that time, however, to date cycles of days, and have been discovered on the earliest Chinese inscriptions yet found, those of the divination bones of the Shang dynasty, dating back probably to as far as 1500 B.C.

The Twelve Earthly Branches have also served another purpose, which has been to mark the points of the compass. Because of this they have also been used to designate the twelve two-hour periods into which the Chinese day was formerly divided before the introduction of western chronology. This is because, according to Chinese ideas, the sun does not rise and set in an orbit approximately perpendicular to the axis of the earth, but rather describes a circle through the sky overhead, which takes it through all the points of the compass. Hence " in spring and autumn, when day and night are nearly of equal length, between 5-7 a.m., the sun stands in, or passes through, *mao*= East, whence the hour from 5-7 a.m. is called the *mao* hour. At noon, 11-1 p.m., it passes through *wu*=South, between 5-7 p.m. through *yu*=West, and at midnight, from 11-1 a.m., the sun, though not seen by us, traverses *tse*=North." [1] The following diagram gives the complete series. In this diagram are also given the names of the twelve animals of the duodenary cycle. Each of these animals corresponds

---

[1] *Cf.* A. Forke, *World Conception of the Chinese*, p. 284.

to one of the two-hour periods, so that Chinese sometimes speak of the hour of the rat, of the ox, etc. These animals are generally supposed to be of Turkish origin, though this has not been definitely proved.

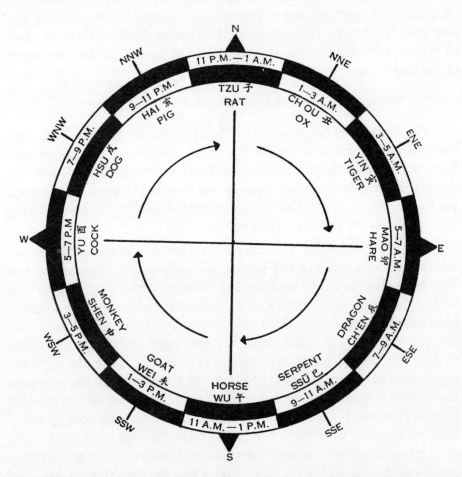

DIAGRAM OF CHINESE DUODENARY HOURS AND COMPASS POINTS

APPENDIX B

PRINCIPAL ANNUAL CHINESE FESTIVALS

Chinese Calendar	Name	Pages in Text
1st of 1st month	New Year's Day (*Yüan Tan* 元旦.). Occurs between Jan. 21 and Feb. 19	.. 1-2,100-105
15th of 1st „	Lantern Festival (*Teng Chieh* 燈節). A nature worship?	.. 6-9
16th of 2nd „ (about)	Festival of Pure Brightness (*Ch'ing Ming* 清明). About April 5. Ancestral	26-27
5th of 5th „	Dragon Boat or 'Upright Sun' Festival (*Tuan Yang Chieh* 端陽節). Nature worship ..	42-45
15th of 7th „	All Souls' Day (*Chung Yüan* 中元). Buddhist and ancestral	60-62
15th of 8th „	Moon or 'Mid-Autumn' Festival (*Chung Ch'iu* 中秋). Nature worship	64-68
9th of 9th „	Hill-climbing or 'Double Ninth' Festival. (*Ch'ung Yang* 重陽). Nature worship?	69-71
1st of 10th „	Time of sending winter clothes to ancestors (*Sung Han I* 送寒衣). Ancestral	.. 75
8th of 12th „	Eighth day of the twelfth month gruel (*La Pa Chou* 臘八粥). Offering made to ancestors, Buddha, etc., as thanksgiving for good harvests	.. 93-94

LISTS OF THE FIRE-CRACKERS, PIGEONS, POPULAR FORMS OF ENTERTAINMENT, SWEET MELONS, CRICKETS, AND CHRYSANTHEMUMS MENTIONED IN THE TEXT

In the following lists, the translator has attempted to give English equivalents for the Chinese names, but in the cases of Crickets and Popular Forms of Entertainment, this has for the most part been found impossible, and therefore explanations of the terms, rather than translations, have been given.   It is extremely difficult to put certain Chinese names into suitable English, so that the translator begs indulgence for any slips he may have committed.

I—Fire-Crackers

These appear in the text under the section on the Lantern Festival in the First Month (p. 7).

Ch'i huo 旂 火 —Flags of fire.

Chin p'an 金 盤 —Golden plates (i.e., pin-wheels).

Erh t'i chiao 二 踢 脚 —Double-kicking feet (i.e., fire-crackers which explode once on the ground, and then again in the air).

Fei t'ien shih hsiang 飛 天 十 響 —Ten explosions flying to heaven.

Ho tzŭ 盒 子 —Small boxes.

Hsien ch'üan mu tan 線 穿 牡 丹 —Peonies strung on a thread.

Hua p'en 花 盆 —Flower pots.

Huo shu 火 樹 —Fire trees.

Lo yüeh 落 月 —Falling moons.

Pa chiao tzŭ 八 角 子 —Eight-cornered rockets.

P'ao ta hsiang yang ch'eng 炮 打 裏 陽 城 —Bombs for attacking the city of Hsiang Yang (a city on the Han River in Hupeh which has always occupied a very important strategic position).[1]

P'u t'ao chia 葡 萄 架 —Grape arbors.

Shui chiao lien 水 澆 蓮 —Lotus sprinkled with water.

T'ien ti teng 天 地 燈 —Lanterns of heaven and earth.

[1] This is undoubtedly a reference to the famous siege of the city by the Mongols in 1268-73, when explosive weapons were used. [Duyvendak]

Wu kuei nao p'an 五 鬼 鬧 判—Five devils noisily splitting apart.

Yen huo kan tzǔ 烟 火 杆 子—Smoke and fire poles (i.e., rockets).

Yin hua 銀 花—Silver flowers.

II—Pigeons

These appear in the text under the section on the Flower Market in the First Month (pp. 21 f.).

1. Ordinary Varieties

Feng t'ou pai 鳳 頭 白—Phœnix-headed white.

Hsi ch'iao hua 喜 鵲 花—Magpie flowers.

Hsiao hui tsao-er 小 灰 皂 兒—Small ash-black.

Hsüeh hua 雪 花—Snow flowers.

Hua pu tzǔ 花 脖 子—Flowery-necked.

Ken t'ou 跟 頭—Heel and head.

Liang t'ou wu 兩 頭 烏—Two-headed black.

Ssǔ k'uai yü 四 塊 玉—Four-piece jade.

Tao shih mao 道 士 帽—Taoist priest hat.

Tien tzǔ 點 子—Dotted.

Tzǔ chiang 紫 醬—Purple sauce.

Yin wei tzǔ 銀 尾 子—Silver-tailed.

Yü ch'ih 玉 翅—Jade-winged.

2. Valuable Varieties

Ch'an yen hui 蟾 眼 灰—Toad-eyed grey.

Ch'i hsing fu 七 星 鳧—Wild duck of the Great Dipper.

Ch'ing mao 青 毛—Azure plumage.

Hao hsiu 鶴 秀—Crane's elegance.

Lan p'an 藍 盤—Blue plate.

Leng ch'i lin 楞 麒 麟—Square-edged unicorn.

Lu ssǔ pai 鷺 鷥 白—Egret-white.

Pan li 斑 跰—Striped sandals.

Pei ma 背 麻—Mottled back.

Pei t'ung 背 銅—Bronze back.

Pei yin 背 銀—Silver back.

T'ieh ch'ih 鐵 翅—Iron-winged.

T'ieh niu 鐵 牛—Iron ox.

Tuan tsui pai 短 嘴 白—Short-beaked white.

Tzŭ tien tzŭ 紫 點 子—Purple-dotted.

Tzŭ wu 紫 烏—Purple-black.

Tzŭ yü ch'ih 紫 玉 翅—Purple jade wings.

Wu niu 烏 牛—Black ox.

Wu t'ou 烏 頭—Black head.

Ying tsui pai 鸚 嘴 白—Parrot-beak white.

Ying tsui tien tzŭ 鸚 嘴 點 子—Parrot-beak spotted.

Yü huan 玉 環—Jade circlet.

Yün p'an 雲 盤—Cloud plate.

III—POPULAR FORMS OF ENTERTAINMENT

These appear in the text under the section on Itinerant Player Societies in the Fifth Month (p. 46), and that on the Closing of the Theatres in the Twelfth Month (pp. 95-97). Those listed under the first group are strictly amateur, whereas those listed under the second are professional.

Chung fan 中 幡—Those who carry the banners for an itinerant player society.

Hsiang sheng 像 聲—Sound imitators.

K'ai lu 開 路—Men dressed up as spiritual beings who form the vanguard of an itinerant player society, and thus serve much the same purpose as the paper figures of spirits which head a funeral procession.

Kang hsiang kuan-er 槓 箱 官 兒—The man who has charge of the boxes and baggage of an itinerant player society, while on a temple pilgrimage, and who is dressed up humorously like an important official, and carried in a crude sedan chair.

Kao ch'iao yang ko 高 蹻 秧 歌—Stilt walkers who sing songs at temple festivals.

K'ua ku hua po 跨 鼓 花 鈸—Those members of an itinerant player society who beat drums and cymbals.

K'uei lei tzŭ 傀 儡 子—also called *t'o hou* (not *ou*) 托 禺—Puppets.

Pa chiao ku 八 角 鼓—Tambourines, i.e., a group of men, some of whom sing and some of whom play stringed instruments and beat tambourines.

Pa shih 把 式—Military arts, such as sword dancing, etc.

P'ing shu 評 書—Story-teller.

Shih pu hsien 什 不 閒—Composed of five persons with gongs, castanets, and drum, who dance and sing ballads.

Shua shih tzŭ 耍 獅 子—Men who dress up as lions and prance and perform acrobatic feats like lions, at temple fairs, etc.

Shua t'an 耍 壜—Performers who juggle and balance large kegs with their legs.

Ta ku 大 鼓—Big drum, i.e., singing and dancing done by female performers.

Tsa shua 雜 耍—also called *pien hsi fa-er* 變 戲 法 兒—Miscellaneous entertainments, i.e., something like our vaudeville or " variety."

Tzŭ ti shu 子 弟 書—Amateur singers who go in groups to the houses of friends, temple festivals, etc.

Wu hu kun 五 虎 棍—Members of an itinerant player society who perform military deeds, etc.

Ying hsi 影 戲—Shadow plays.

IV—SWEET MELONS

These appear in the text under the Fifth Month (p. 52).

Ch'ing p'i ts'ui 青 皮 脆—Green-skin crushables.

Ha mi su 哈 密 酥—Hami crisps (Hami is a place in Chinese Turkestan).

Han chin chui 旱 金 墜—Dry golden droppers.

Lao t'ou-er lo 老 頭 兒 樂—Old man's delight.

Wei kua jang 倭 瓜 瓤—Wei pulps (Wei is a place in Chinese Turkestan).

Yang chiao mi 羊 角 蜜—Sheep-horn honey.

V—CRICKETS

The first name listed appears under the Seventh Month (p. 63), the remainder under the section on Crickets in the Tenth Month (pp. 81-83).

Chin chung-er 金 鐘 兒—Little golden bells (*homeogryllus japonicus*).

Kua kua-er 聒 聒 兒—ie., " noisy ones," a general term for crickets.

Lao mi tsui 老 米 嘴—Old rice mandibles. These have sharp jaws.

Pang tzŭ t'ou 梆 子 頭—Clothes-beater heads. These have large heads. The *pang tzŭ* is a small wooden truncheon used by Chinese women to beat clothes while washing them.

Yu hu lu 油 壺 盧—i.e., " oily " *hu-lu*. These are fat, large, and have a rich color like oil.

Chü chü-er 蚰 蚰 兒—also called *hsi shuai* 蟀 蟋—These are found from the seventh month onward, and include :

1. *Chu chieh hsü* 竹 節 鬚—Bamboo-joint whiskers.
2. *Hsieh kai ch'ing* 蟹 蓋 青—Crab-shell green.
3. *Huang ma t'ou* 黃 麻 頭—Yellow-mottled heads.
4. *Mei hua ch'ih* 梅 花 翅—Plum-flower winged.
5. *Pai ma t'ou* 白 麻 頭—White-mottled heads.
6. *P'i pa ch'ih* 琵 琶 翅—*P'i-pa*-winged (the *p'i-pa* is a kind of guitar).

VI—CHRYSANTHEMUMS

These appear in the section on Chrysanthemum Hillocks under the Ninth Month (pp. 71-73), where it is said that they fall under four classifications : Those having last year's stalks (*ch'en yang* 陳 秧), i.e., which are more than one year old ; those having this year's stalks (*hsin yang* 新 秧), i.e., ones newly grown this year ; the fine (*hsi* 細) variety ; and the coarse (*ts'u* 粗) variety. As far as actual appearance of the flowers is concerned, there seems to be no valid distinction between those of last year's stalks, and those of this year's. The fine variety, however, is that of chrysanthemums having petals which are thin and threadlike, curling at the tips, whereas those of the coarse variety have broad petals.

Chrysanthemums, together with the peony and lotus, are perhaps the best loved flowers in China (because, for one reason, they are the last to bloom, and can resist the cold after all else is dead), and rich Chinese gentlemen frequently have exhibitions of them to which guests are annually invited. A great amount of imagination is used in naming them, and these names well display the typical Chinese delight in elaborate imagery. Hence a list is given here, although it must be remembered that names for chrysanthemums differ greatly according to their period, and according to the whim of individuals, who think up different names to give to new freak flower specimens which they have developed. For this reason probably few of the names given by our author will be found in common use to-day. Some of his total of one hundred and thirty-three varieties have been omitted here, because it has been found almost impossible to render them into intelligible English.

1. LAST YEAR'S STALKS OF THE FINE VARIETY

Ch'ang yü lou 長 玉 樓—Long jade hall.

Chia sha 袈 裟—Priest's robe.

Ch'ieh lan 茄 藍—Egg-plant blue.

Chin su 金 素—Gold unadorned.

Ch'ing ho lien 青 河 蓮—Azure water-lily.

Ch'ing lien tzŭ 青 蓮 子—Azure lotus.

Ch'ing shan kai hsüeh 青 山 蓋 雪—Snow-covered azure mountain.

Chu pan 朱 辦—Red petalled.

Chu sha kai hsüeh 硃 砂 蓋 雪—Snow-covered cinnabar.

Ch'un hsiao pao ch'a 春 曉 寶 刹—Precious monastery of the spring dawn.

Fang chin yin 方 金 印—Square golden seal.

Fou t'u lo hung 浮 圖 落 紅—Buddhist red.

Hsi shih hsiao chuang 西 施 曉 妝—Radiant beauty of Hsi Shih (a famous beauty of the fifth century B.C.).

Hsiang lien 湘 蓮—Hsiang River lotus.

Hsiao hsiang fei tzŭ 瀟 湘 妃 子—Concubine of the Hsiao and Hsiang Rivers.

Hsing lin ch'un yen 杏 林 春 燕—Spring swallow in an apricot orchard.

Hui hao ch'ih 灰 鶴 翅—Ash-crane wings.

I shang 霓 裳—Rainbow-skirted.

Lao chün mei 老 君 眉—Eyebrows of the Old Ruler (i.e., the Taoist sage, Lao Tzŭ).

Mi chin kuan 米 金 管—Rice-gold duct.

Mi lien huan 蜜 連 環—Honey linked-bracelets.

Ô ling kuan 鵝 翎 管—Goose quills.

Pai hao wo hsüeh 白 鶴 臥 雪—White crane sleeping in the snow.

P'ing sha lo yen 平 沙 落 雁—Wild goose settling on level sand.

T'ao hua shan 桃 花 扇—Peach-blossom fan.

T'ao hung 桃 紅—Peach-red.

Teng ts'ao kuan 燈 草 管—Lamp-wick duct.

Tzŭ hu hsü 紫 虎 鬚—Purple tiger-whiskers.

Wan tien ni chin 萬 點 泥 金—Clay-speckled gold.

Wan tien ou se 萬 點 鵝 色—Speckled lotus-root color.

Yin hung chen 銀 紅 針—Silver-red needle.

Yü ch'ih 玉 池—Jade pool.

Yü sun 玉 筍—Jade shoots.

2. LAST YEAR'S STALKS OF THE COARSE VARIETY

Chin feng ling 金 鳳 翎—Golden phœnix wings.

Chin hsia huan 金 霞 環—Gold mist bracelets.

Chin lien huan 金 連 環—Gold linked-bracelets.

Chin mao shih tzŭ 金 毛 獅 子—Golden-hair lion.

Chin p'an hsien lu 金 盤 獻 露—Golden plate presenting dew (see note on p. 72).

Erh se lien 二 色 蓮—Two-colored lotus.

Fen mu tan 粉 牡 丹—Variegated peony.

Fen p'ing 粉 屏—Decorated screen.

Feng lin lo chao 楓 林 落 照—Radiance falling from a maple forest (i.e., maple leaves falling in the autumn ?).

Fu jung ch'iu yen 芙 蓉 秋 豔—Autumn beauty of the hibiscus.

Han ti chin lien 旱 地 金 蓮—Dry-land golden lotus (i.e., probably a Chinese lady's bound foot, this being euphemistically called " golden lotus ").

Hsi yang hsieh chao 夕 陽 斜 照—Oblique light of the evening sun.

Hsiao t'ien hsia lan 曉 天 霞 藍—Blue of mist at break of day.

Hsin chin k'uei 滲 金 葵—Dripping-gold sunflower.

Hsing kuang tsai shui 星 光 在 水—Starlight in the water.

Hsü chia tzŭ 徐 家 紫—Purple of the Hsü family.

Huang hao mao 黃 鶴 毛—Yellow crane feathers.

Lan ling chiu 藍 翎 九—Blue-winged nine.

Lu hao mao 鷺 鶴 毛—Egret-crane feathers.

Pai mu tan 白 牡 丹—White peony.

Ta chin k'uei 大 金 葵—Great golden sunflower.

Ta hung pao chu 大 紅 寶 珠—Big red precious pearl.

Tzŭ feng shu ling 紫 鳳 舒 翎—Outstretched wings of purple phœnix.

Tzŭ hsieh chao 紫 蟹 爪—Purple crab claws.

Ts'ang lung hsü 蒼 龍 鬚—Azure dragon-whiskers.

Ts'ang lung hsün tzŭ 蒼 龍 訓 子—Azure dragon teaching his sons.

Tzŭ lung k'ai chao 紫 龍 開 爪—Purple dragon with open claws.

Tzŭ mu tan 紫 牡 丹—Purple peony.

Tzŭ sung chen 紫 松 針—Purple pine-needle.

Ya pei hsi yang 鴉 背 夕 陽—Evening sun on a duck's back.

Yin chen 銀 針—Silver needle.

Ying jih ho hua 映 日 河 花—Lily on a dazzling day.

Yü ch'ih tiao keng 玉 匙 調 羹—Jade spoon stirring broth.

Yü shan 玉 扇—Jade fan.

Yün lung huan ts'ai 雲 龍 煥 彩—Lustrous variegated cloud-dragon.

3. THIS YEAR'S STALKS OF THE FINE VARIETY

Chin chüan chu sha 金 捲 硃 砂—Cinnabar rolled up in gold.

Chin feng han chu 金 鳳 含 珠—Golden phœnix holding a pearl in its mouth.

Chin ju i 金 如 意—Gold as one likes it.

Ch'ung yang chü chu 重 陽 居 住—Two suns together.

Ch'iu shui fu jung 秋 水 芙 蓉—Hibiscus of autumn waters.

Ch'iu shui ming hsia 秋 水 明 霞—Clear mist on autumn waters.

Chu hsia 朱 霞—Red mist.

Chu mo shuang hui 硃 墨 雙 輝—Red-and-black double radiance.

Erh ch'iao cheng yen 二 喬 爭 豔—Two proud persons vying in beauty.

Feng kuan 鳳 管—Phœnix flute.

Han kung ch'un hsiao 漢 宮 春 曉—Spring dawn at the Han palace.

Hsiang pai li 香 白 梨 —Fragrant white pear.

Hsien jen chang 仙 人 掌—Immortal's palms.

Huan hua hsi 浣 花 溪—Flowers washed at a brook.

Huang hao hsien jen 黃 鶴 仙 人—Yellow crane Immortal.

Huang hsiu ch'iu 黃 繡 球—Yellow geranium.

Kao ch'iu ta fu 羔 裘 大 夫—Official in lamb's fur.

Luan sheng 鸞 笙—*Luan* bird (a fabulous bird) reed-organ.

Ling yang kua chiao 羚 羊 挂 角—Hung-up horns of the antelope.

Liu hsien ch'ui chin 柳 線 垂 金—Willow streamers drooping gold.

Mo hu hsü 墨 虎 鬚—Black tiger-whiskers.

Nan chi hsien weng 南 極 仙 翁—Ancient Immortal of the south pole.

Niao chao hsien jen 鳥 爪 仙 人—Bird's talon Immortal.

Shan hu kou 珊 瑚 鉤—Red-coral hook.

Shui ching ju i 水 晶 如 意—Quartzcrystal as one likes it.

Shui t'ien pan 水 天 半—Half-water half-sky.

T'ao hua jen mien 桃 花 人 面—Peach blossom with a human face.

T'ien nü san hua 天 女 散 花—Heavenly Maid (i.e., Spinning Maiden) scattering flowers.

Tsui t'ai po 醉 太 白—Intoxicated T'ai Po (i.e., Li T'ai Po, 705 ?-762, China's greatest poet, who was also noted for his fondness for the bottle).

Yang hu tieh 洋 蝴 蝶—Ocean butterfly.

Yin hu hsü 銀 虎 鬚—Silver tiger-whiskers.

4. THIS YEAR'S STALKS OF THE COARSE VARIETY

Ch'i lin ying ko 麒 麟 鸚 哥—Unicorn and parrot.

Chin fo tso 金 佛 座—Golden Buddha seat.

Chin kou kua yü 金 鈎 挂 玉—Jade suspended from a golden hook.

Chin pien ta hung 金 邊 大 紅—Big-red with golden border.

Ho chia huan. lo 合 家 歡 樂—A good time being had by a united family.

Hsi shih fen 西 施 粉—Hsi Shih's face powder.

Lü liu huang li 綠 柳 黃 鸝—Yellow orioles in the green willows.

Mi feng wo 蜜 蜂 窩—Beehive.

Pao tzŭ 抱 子—Embracing a child.

Tzŭ p'ao chin tai 紫 袍 金 帶—Purple jacket with golden belt.

Tzŭ shou chin chang 紫 綬 金 章—Purple ribbon and golden seal.

Tzŭ tien ch'ing shuang 紫 電 青 霜—Purple lightning and azure frost.

Yang fei tsui wu 楊 妃 醉 舞—Intoxicated Yang Kuei-fei dancing (she was the consort of Emperor Ming Huang, who reigned 712-756, and China's most famous beauty).

Yü t'ang chin ma 玉 堂 金 馬—Jade hall with a golden horse.

APPENDIX D

CHINESE UNITS OF MEASUREMENT

Length:

The Chinese foot (*ch'ih* 尺) is of various types and sizes, but as fixed by treaty for international trade purposes, is 14.1 English inches. It contains ten Chinese inches (*ts'un* 寸), while ten *ch'ih* make one *chang* 丈. About three *li* 里 are equivalent to one English mile.

Weight:

The catty (*chin* 斤) is equivalent to 1⅓ English pounds, and contains sixteen ounces (*liang* 兩). A *tan* 石, when used as a unit of weight, is equal to 100 catties.

Capacity:

A pint (*sheng* 升) is equal to 1.03 litres. Ten *sheng* equal one peck (*tou* 斗), and ten *tou* equal one *tan* 石, which hence is equivalent to 1.03 hectolitres.

Currency:

The tael is one Chinese ounce of silver, but has varied greatly in different parts of the country. In the old days 1,000 copper cash strung together to make one " string " (*tiao* 吊 or *min* 緡) of cash were supposed to equal one tael. Actually, however, such a string was usually many short of the required number of 1,000 cash.

PRINCIPAL CHINESE DYNASTIES AND SOME OF THE EMPERORS AND REIGN TITLES

Hsia 夏	... 2205 ?-1766 ? B.C.
Shang 商	... 1765 ?-1123 ? B.C.
Chou 周	... 1122 ?-255 B.C.
Ch'in 秦	... 255-207 B.C.
Han 漢	... 206 B.C.-A.D. 220
Three Kingdoms 三 國	... 220-280
Six Dynasties 六 朝	... 265-589
Sui 隋	... 589-618
T'ang 唐	... 618-906
Five Dynasties 五 代	... 907-960
*Liao 遼	... 907-1124
Sung 宋	... 960-1279
*Chin 金	... 1115-1234
Yüan 元 (Mongol)	... 1280-1368

Genghis Khan (T'ai Tsu 太 祖) 1206-1227
Reigned before the Mongols had completely conquered China.

Kublai Khan (Shih Tsu 世 祖) 1260-1294
Actually seated himself on throne of China in 1280.

Ming 明 1368-1644

Hung Wu 洪 武 1368-1398
Chien Wen 建 文 1399-1402
Yung Lo 永 樂 1403-1424
Hung Hsi 洪 熙 1425
Hsüan Te 宣 德 1426-1435

---

* These were Tartar dynasties, and not recognized by the Chinese as legitimate, but are important in the history of Peking, since they ruled the territory where Peking now stands.

Cheng T'ung 正統 1436-1449
Ching T'ai 景泰 1450-1456
T'ien Shun 天順 1457-1464
Ch'eng Hua 成化 1465-1487
Hung Chih 弘治 1488-1505
Cheng Te 正德 1506-1521
Chia Ching 嘉靖 1522-1566
Lung Ch'ing 隆慶 1567-1572
Wan Li 萬曆 1573-1620
T'ai Ch'ang 泰昌 1620
T'ien Ch'i 天啓 1621-1627
Ch'ung Cheng 崇禎 1628-1644

CH'ING 清 (MANCHU) 1644-1912

Shun Chih 順治 1644-1661
K'ang Hsi 康熙 1662-1722
Yung Cheng 雍正 1723-1735
Ch'ien Lung 乾隆 1736-1795
Chia Ch'ing 嘉慶 1796-1820
Tao Kuang 道光 1821-1850
Hsien Feng 咸豐 1851-1861
T'ung Chih 同治 1862-1874
Kuang Hsü 光緒 1875-1908
Hsüan T'ung 宣統 1908-1912

CONCORDANCE OF LUNAR AND WESTERN CALENDARS
FROM 1957 TO 1984

Source: P. Hoang, *Concordance des chronologies néoméniques chinoise et européenne* (Shanghai: Variétés Sinologiques No. 29, 1910)

By using this concordance, one may easily calculate the date in the Western calendar for any festival mentioned in this book during the years 1957 to 1984. In the first column appear the months of the lunar calendar of each year. The asterisk * indicates that that month is intercalary. In the second column appear the dates in the Western calendar upon which the first day of the corresponding lunar month falls. In the parentheses following each year is given the animal of the zodiac for the corresponding lunar year (for which *cf.* also pp. 109-110).

1957 (Cock)		1958 (Dog)		1959 (Pig)		1960 (Rat)	
Lunar	*Western*	*Lunar*	*Western*	*Lunar*	*Western*	*Lunar*	*Western*
12	Jan. 1	12	Jan. 20	12	Jan. 9	1	Jan. 28
1	Jan. 31	1	Feb. 18	1	Feb. 8	2	Feb. 27
2	Mar. 2	2	Mar. 20	2	Mar. 9	3	Mar. 27
3	Mar. 31	3	Apr. 19	3	Apr. 8	4	Apr. 26
4	Apr. 30	4	May 19	4	May 8	5	May 25
5	May 29	5	June 17	5	June 6	6	June 24
6	June 28	6	July 17	6	July 6	*6	July 24
7	July 27	7	Aug. 15	7	Aug. 4	7	Aug. 22
8	Aug. 25	8	Sept. 13	8	Sept. 3	8	Sept. 21
*8	Sept. 24	9	Oct. 13	9	Oct. 2	9	Oct. 20
9	Oct. 23	10	Nov. 11	10	Nov. 1	10	Nov. 19
10	Nov. 22	11	Dec. 11	11	Nov. 30	11	Dec. 18
11	Dec. 21			12	Dec. 30		

1961 (Ox)		1963 (Hare)		1965 (Serpent)		1967 (Sheep)	
Lunar	Western	Lunar	Western	Lunar	Western	Lunar	Western
12	Jan. 17	1	Jan. 25	12	Jan. 3	12	Jan. 11
1	Feb. 15	2	Feb. 24	1	Feb. 2	1	Feb. 9
2	Mar. 17	3	Mar. 25	2	Mar. 3	2	Mar. 11
3	Apr. 15	4	Apr. 24	3	Apr. 2	3	Apr. 10
4	May 15	*4	May 23	4	May 1	4	May 9
5	June 13	5	June 21	5	May 31	5	June 8
6	July 13	6	July 21	6	June 29	6	July 8
7	Aug. 11	7	Aug. 19	7	July 28	7	Aug. 6
8	Sept. 10	8	Sept. 18	8	Aug. 27	8	Sept. 4
9	Oct. 10	9	Oct. 17	9	Sept. 25	9	Oct. 4
10	Nov. 8	10	Nov. 16	10	Oct. 24	10	Nov. 2
11	Dec. 8	11	Dec. 16	11	Nov. 23	11	Dec. 2
				12	Dec. 23	12	Dec. 31

1962 (Tiger)		1964 (Dragon)		1966 (Horse)		1968 (Monkey)	
12	Jan. 6	12	Jan. 15	1	Jan. 21	1	Jan. 30
1	Feb. 5	1	Feb. 13	2	Feb. 20	2	Feb. 28
2	Mar. 6	2	Mar. 14	3	Mar. 22	3	Mar. 29
3	Apr. 5	3	Apr. 12	*3	Apr. 21	4	Apr. 27
4	May 4	4	May 12	4	May 20	5	May 27
5	June 2	5	June 10	5	June 19	6	June 26
6	July 2	6	July 9	6	July 18	7	July 25
7	July 31	7	Aug. 8	7	Aug. 16	*7	Aug. 24
8	Aug. 30	8	Sept. 6	8	Sept. 15	8	Sept. 22
9	Sept. 29	9	Oct. 6	9	Oct. 14	9	Oct. 22
10	Oct. 28	10	Nov. 4	10	Nov. 12	10	Nov. 20
11	Nov. 27	11	Dec. 4	11	Dec. 12	11	Dec. 20
12	Dec. 27						

1969 (Cock)		1971 (Pig)		1973 (Ox)		1975 (Hare)	
Lunar	*Western*	*Lunar*	*Western*	*Lunar*	*Western*	*Lunar*	*Western*
12	Jan. 18	1	Jan. 27	12	Jan. 4	12	Jan. 12
1	Feb. 17	2	Feb. 25	1	Feb. 3	1	Feb. 11
2	Mar. 18	3	Mar. 27	2	Mar. 5	2	Mar. 13
3	Apr. 17	4	Apr. 25	3	Apr. 3	3	Apr. 12
4	May 16	5	May 24	4	May 3	4	May 11
5	June 15	*5	June 23	5	June 1	5	June 10
6	July 14	6	July 22	6	June 30	6	July 9
7	Aug. 13	7	Aug. 21	7	July 30	7	Aug. 7
8	Sept. 12	8	Sept. 19	8	Aug. 28	8	Sept. 6
9	Oct. 11	9	Oct. 19	9	Sept. 26	9	Oct. 5
10	Nov. 10	10	Nov. 18	10	Oct. 26	10	Nov. 3
11	Dec. 9	11	Dec. 18	11	Nov. 25	11	Dec. 3
				12	Dec. 24		

1970 (Dog)		1972 (Rat)		1974 (Tiger)		1976 (Dragon)	
12	Jan. 8	12	Jan. 16	1	Jan. 23	12	Jan. 1
1	Feb. 6	1	Feb. 15	2	Feb. 22	1	Jan. 31
2	Mar. 8	2	Mar. 15	3	Mar. 24	2	Mar. 1
3	Apr. 6	3	Apr. 14	4	Apr. 22	3	Mar. 31
4	May 5	4	May 13	*4	May 22	4	Apr. 29
5	June 4	5	June 11	5	June 20	5	May 29
6	July 3	6	July 11	6	July 19	6	June 27
7	Aug. 2	7	Aug. 9	7	Aug. 18	7	July 27
8	Sept. 1	8	Sept. 8	8	Sept. 16	8	Aug. 25
9	Sept. 30	9	Oct. 7	9	Oct. 15	*8	Sept. 24
10	Oct. 30	10	Nov. 6	10	Nov. 14	9	Oct. 23
11	Nov. 29	11	Dec. 6	11	Dec. 14	10	Nov. 21
12	Dec. 28					11	Dec. 21

1977 (Serpent)		1979 (Sheep)		1981 (Cock)		1983 (Pig)	
Lunar	Western	Lunar	Western	Lunar	Western	Lunar	Western
12	Jan. 19	1	Jan. 28	12	Jan. 6	12	Jan. 14
1	Feb. 18	2	Feb. 27	1	Feb. 5	1	Feb. 13
2	Mar. 20	3	Mar. 28	2	Mar. 6	2	Mar. 15
3	Apr. 18	4	Apr. 26	3	Apr. 5	3	Apr. 13
4	May 18	5	May 26	4	May 4	4	May 13
5	June 17	6	June 24	5	June 2	5	June 11
6	July 16	*6	July 24	6	July 2	6	July 10
7	Aug. 15	7	Aug. 23	7	July 31	7	Aug. 9
8	Sept. 13	8	Sept. 21	8	Aug. 29	8	Sept. 7
9	Oct. 13	9	Oct. 21	9	Sept. 28	9	Oct. 6
10	Nov. 11	10	Nov. 20	10	Oct. 28	10	Nov. 11
11	Dec. 11	11	Dec. 19	11	Nov. 26	11	Dec. 4
				12	Dec. 26		

1978 (Horse)		1980 (Monkey)		1982 (Dog)		1984 (Rat)	
12	Jan. 9	12	Jan. 18	1	Jan. 25	12	Jan. 3
1	Feb. 7	1	Feb. 16	2	Feb. 24	1	Feb. 2
2	Mar. 9	2	Mar. 17	3	Mar. 25	2	Mar. 3
3	Apr. 7	3	Apr. 15	4	Apr. 24	3	Apr. 1
4	May 7	4	May 14	*4	May 23	4	May 1
5	June 6	5	June 13	5	June 21	5	May 31
6	July 5	6	July 12	6	July 21	6	June 29
7	Aug. 4	7	Aug. 11	7	Aug. 19	7	July 28
8	Sept. 2	8	Sept. 9	8	Sept. 17	8	Aug. 27
9	Oct. 2	9	Oct. 9	9	Oct. 17	9	Sept. 25
10	Nov. 1	10	Nov. 8	10	Nov. 15	10	Oct. 24
11	Nov. 30	11	Dec. 7	11	Dec. 15	*10	Nov. 23
12	Dec. 30					11	Dec. 22

BIBLIOGRAPHY

This bibliography has for its purpose simply to bring together those works mentioned by the author in his text. Numbers refer to the pages where they are mentioned. Other books mentioned in the notes by the translator, will be found listed in the Index. No attempt is made here to compile a complete list of western works dealing with the subject of the present book, but among a few of the more useful may be mentioned:

ADAM, Maurice, *Us et Coutumes de la région de Pékin d'après le Je Sia Kieu Wen K'ao, Ch. 146-147-148*, Peiping, 1930.

ARLINGTON and LEWISOHN, *In Search of Old Peking*, Peiping, 1935.

BOGAN, M. L. C., *Manchu Customs and Superstitions*, Tientsin-Peking, 1928.

BREDON and MITROPHANOW, *The Moon Year, a Record of Chinese Customs and Festivals*, Shanghai, 1927.

DE GROOT, J. J. M., *Les fêtes annuellement célébrées à Emoui (Amoy) : étude concernant la religion populaire des Chinois*, 2 vols., Paris, 1886.

DORÉ, Henri, S.J., *Recherches sur les superstitions en Chine*, 16 vols., Shanghai, 1911-1929, English ed. translated by Kenelly, 10 vols., Shanghai, 1914-1926.[1]

GRUBE, Wilhelm, *Zur Pekinger Volkskunde*, Berlin, 1901.

SHYROCK, John, *The Temples of Anking and their Cults*, Paris, 1931.

WERNER, E. T. C., *A Dictionary of Chinese Mythology*, Shanghai, 1932.

CHINESE WORKS REFERRED TO BY THE AUTHOR:

Ch'en-yüan Shih-lüeh 宸垣識略, by Wu Ch'ang-yüan 吳長元, 16 *chüan*, about 1786. A descriptive work of the surroundings of Peking: 10, 49, 56.

Chi-yüan-chi-so-chi 寄園寄所寄, compiled by Chao Chi-shih 趙吉士 in 1659, 12 *chüan*. A collection of accounts and stories dealing chiefly with the Ming dynasty. The information it contains is often fanciful and shows lack of discrimination (*cf.* Wylie, p. 171): 74.

[1] Since 1936 when the first edition of this work appeared, Doré's opus has been extended to a final total of 18 volumes (Shanghai 1911-1938), and Kennelly's English translation to 13 volumes (Shanghai 1914-1938). See also *Manuel des Superstitions chinoises, ou petit indicateur des superstitions les plus communes en Chine*, by P. H. Doré, S.J., Shanghai 1926.

Ching-ch'u Sui-shih-chi 荆楚歲時記, by Tsung Lin 宗懍, (*ca.* 500—*ca.* 563), 1 *chüan*. A calendar of popular customs throughout the year (*cf.* Wylie, *Notes on Chinese Literature*, p. 56): 1, 51.

Chü-i-lu 居易錄, by Wang Shih-cheng 王士禎 (1634-1711), 34 *chüan*. Written 1689-1701, dealing with poetry, etc.: 21.

Feng-su-t'ung-i 風俗通義, by Ying Shao 應劭 of latter part of second century A.D., 10 *chüan*, supplement 1 *chüan*. Written to rectify decadence which had taken place in popular customs (*cf.* Wylie, p. 163): 45.

Han Shu 漢書, by Pan Ku 班固 (died A.D. 92), 100 *chüan*. The dynastic history of the Former Han dynasty (206 B.C.-A.D. 24), (*cf.* Wylie, pp. 16 f.): 87.

Hou Han Shu 後漢書, by Fan Yeh 范曄 (died A.D. 445), 120 *chüan*. The dynastic history of the Later Han dynasty (A.D. 25-220), (*cf.* Wylie, pp. 16 f.): 44.

Hsi-ching-chih-tien 析津志典, by Hsiung Meng-hsiang 熊夢祥 (lived somewhere around A.D. 1335): 27, 71, 76.

Hsü-ch'i-hsieh-chi 續齊諧記, by Wu Chün 吳均 (469-520), 1 *chüan*. A short record of marvels (*cf.* Wylie, p. 193): 42.

*I-ch'ing-ko Tsa-ch'ao 倚晴閣雜抄: 90.

Jih-hsia Chiu-wen-k'ao 日下舊聞考, 160 *chüan*, a detailed revision undertaken in 1774 in accordance with Imperial order, of the earlier *Jih-hsia Chiu-wen* 日下舊聞 by Chu I-tsun 朱彝尊. Referred to in the text as *Jih-hsia*. The most important work for archæological and historical information about Peking and its environs (*cf.* Wylie, p. 44): 8, 15, 16, 18, 20, 32, 34, 36, 37, 38, 47, 50, 58, 59, 61, 69, 70, 78, 79, 80, 81, 83, 90, 98, 102, 105.

Kuang-ch'ün-fang-p'u 廣羣芳譜, 100 *chüan*, a revision undertaken under royal patronage in 1708 of the *Ch'ün-fang-p'u* 羣芳譜 by Wang Hsiang-chin 王象晉 of end of Ming. A work on agriculture (*cf.* Wylie, p. 152): 94.

---

* See Note on next page.

Li-pu Tse-li 禮部則例, by Te Pao 德保 and others, 194 *chüan*, 1784. A work on government organization : 5.

*Pei-ching Sui-hua-chi 北京歲華記 :xxviii, 11, 75.

P'i Ya 埤雅, by Lu Tien 陸佃 (1042-1102), 20 *chüan*. A philological work which investigates the origins of miscellaneous terms and ceremonies : 50.

Shih-shih Yao-lan 釋氏要覽, compiled by Buddhist priest Tao Ch'eng 道誠 of Sung, 3 *chüan* : 62.[†]

Shih-wu Yüan-hui 事物原會, by Wang Chi 汪汲, 14 *chüan*, preface dated 1796-1797. Gives origins of things and customs : 92.

*Sui-shih Pai-wen 歲時百問 : 27.

Ti-ching Ching-wu-lüeh 帝京景物略, by Liu T'ung 劉侗 and Yü I-cheng 于奕正, 8 *chüan*, 1635. An important early descriptive work of Peking and its environs :xxviii, 4, 56, 66, 71, 75, 79, 89, 98.

Yen-tu Yu-lan-chih 燕都遊覽志, by Sun Kuo-chuang 孫國莊 of Ming, 40 *chüan*. A book of observations on Peking : 93.[†]

Yü-chu Pao-tien 玉燭寶典, by Tu T'ai-ch'ing 杜臺卿 (died *ca*. A.D. 575), 12 *chüan*. An almanac of the year : 2.

*Yü-shih Pien-lin 余氏辨林: 22.

Yüeh Ling 月令, now one of Chapters in *Li Chi* (Legge, *Sacred Books of the East*, XXVII, 249-310). Also found in earlier *Lü-shih Ch'un Ch'iu* 呂氏春秋, compiled under Lü Pu-wei 呂不韋 (died B.C. 235). One of oldest Chinese almanacs : 19.

Yüeh-ling Kuang-i 月令廣義, by Feng Ying-ching 馮應京, who became a *chin shih* in 1592, 25 *chüan*. An almanac of the year, containing many legends and strange stories : 25.[†]

---

* Though these works are referred to in the *Jih-hsia Chiu-wen-k'ao*, I have been unable to find trace of them either in the *Combined Indices to Twenty History Bibliographies* or the *Index to Ssŭ K'u Ch'üan Shu Tsung Mu and Wei Shou Shu Mu* (Harvard-Yenching Institute Sinological Index Series, Nos. 7 and 10). Neither have the National Library of Peiping, or Dean William Hung of the Harvard-Yenching Institute at Yenching University, been able to give me information concerning them. They are perhaps lost works, or works existing only as fragments quoted in other works.

†See corrigenda and explanations in the Introduction to the Second Edition, p. xix

INDEX

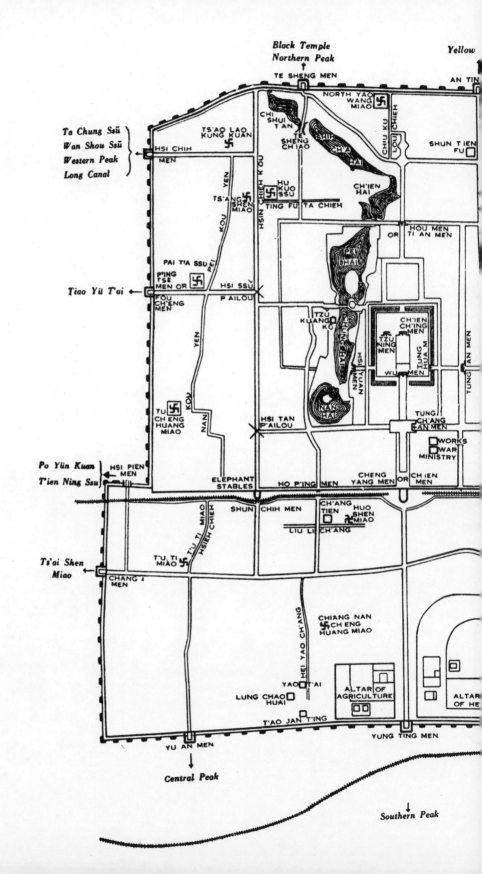